Typos & Awl

Selections from a Humor Blog

By Brad Hollerbach

Typos & Awl
Selections from a Humor Blog
by Brad Hollerbach

December 2010

Patches
PUBLICATIONS

Thanks to Joe, James, Mark, and Mike for often being unsuspecting sounding boards for a number of ideas that eventually became blogs.

Thanks to Jon and Rex Rust and the Southeast Missourian for allowing free-range "community bloggers" to exist on its website.

And to the visitors to SEMISSOURIAN.COM who've enjoyed my blogs, I sincerely say, thanks for reading.

This book is dedicated to:

Karie
who embraces (most of) my eccentricities,

Mom & Dad
who live without the Internet and therefore
have a very difficult time reading online blogs,

and to Patches,
who would rather I move the damn laptop
so I could do more important things like scratch her chin.

Table of Contents

Introduction	7
Becoming Canadian	8
A Letter From Murray McOinkers	10
Does A Flashlight Need An 8-Page Manual?	12
Ralph The Terrorist	13
An Email From Nicole Brown	15
Indoor Hunting	17
"Erosion" A New Concept For Corp of Engineers	19
I Are My Own Proof Reader.	21
Incontinent Donuts Need Federal Grant	22
Medical Diagnosis Via Phone App? ¡NOFREAKINWAY!	23
Dear Doofuses Sightseeing After The Ice Storm	25
The Death of Buckwheat The Second	26
Haz-Mat Gardening License Optional	28
Health Insurance Form Letter Deserves 'Filing'	30
How to Write a Blog In FOUR EASY STEPS!	32
Sheep Burping Research	35
Dear Doofus In The White Buick At The ATM	37
'Old School' Heating	38
HCR 99 – Saluting the Reese's Peanut Butter Egg	40
I Don't Get 'The Rich'	42
This Blog Is For The Birds	43
Burglar-Proofing Your Home With Bert And Ernie	44
Economic Impact BULLSHEET	46
Magazine 'Free Gift' Leaves Something To Be Desired	48
Logging Reality Shows Have Room For One More	49
Dear Doofus in the Camaro on Route K	51
'Personal and Confidential' Mail Is Anything But	52
'Bazooka Joe' Covertly Corrupting Our Youth	54
I Am No Longer A 'Blogger'	56
Where Does Pepperoni Come From?	59
Don't Like A Definition? Try a Different Dictionary.	61
Getting Rid Of Grandpa Franklin	63

Table of Contents

Soda Additives Anonymous **65**

It's Tough To Legislate Ugly **66**

Dear Doofus Who Rented "The DaVinci Code" Before Me **68**

KFC 'Honey' Is Not What It Seems **70**

TPing In The Good Ol' Days **71**

A Surplus Of Left-Handed Work Gloves **72**

The Never-Ending War **73**

The Canadians Are Coming! The Canadians Are Coming! **74**

The Forecast Calls For.... A Tsunami???? **77**

Whatever Happened To Quality? **79**

Shouldn't Baristas Be Really, Really, <u>Really</u> Fast? **81**

'Crop Circle' Proof Of Alien Invasion **82**

The Second Annual Christmas Running of the Cats **84**

Just Where Is THE Meth Capital? **86**

Hating My Bank **88**

Is It Wrong To Love My Trashcan? **90**

'Clunkers For Cruisers' **92**

Dear Anal-Retentive Snow Plow Operator **94**

Is 'Stupid' a Pre-Existing Condition? **96**

Lost Pet. Brown With Curly Hair. Weighs One Ton. **98**

An Outhouse With A Bad Mullet **100**

Smoking Bans Don't Go Far Enough **102**

The 'Fighting Smileys' of Wal-Mart U. **104**

Welcome To The Bank Of Brad **106**

'G****** Zhu Zhu Robotic Hamsters' **108**

The Bogey-Committee **110**

Things I have in common with the Tasmanian Devil **112**

Why I've Never Been A Cow **113**

The Adolf Hitler Campbell Trilogy **114**

Church Foreclosures On The Rise **118**

A Blog Where I Don't Complain **119**

When Ants Won't Eat The Cat Food **121**

Dear Doofus 'Parked' In The Passing Lane **123**

Introduction

This is a collection of essays I've written since November 2008 that have appeared at *The Irony Of It All* blog on the *SEMissourian.com* website.

Unfortunately, since I have been both the writer and editor of these submissions, they have featured a number of typos, errors, grammatical faux pas, poor grammar, redundancies, comma splices, dangling participles, split infinitives and a whole lot of run on sentences that just never, ever seem to want to ever want to stop, ever.

Sorry.

I've tried to correct the most glaring of those problems while assembling this compilation.

When I decided to create this collection, I was initially planning on re-working some of the entries. I'm a bit of a tinkerer and a DIYer, and as my wife would tell you, I'm never ever done with anything.

But on further reflection, I decided to do very little editing or revising. These blogs were written at a specific point in time and so they shall remain. They made me laugh when I wrote them and laugh again when I was deciding which ones to include in this collection.

Thank you for buying this book.

And thanks for reading.

Becoming Canadian

Originally Posted Wednesday, January 7, 2009

Russian Professor Igor Panarin is predicting that the U.S. will have a civil war this coming fall and dissolve into six entities by the summer of 2010.

According to the *Wall Street Journal*, he posits that "a mass immigration, economic decline, and moral degradation" will trigger the breakup of the United States.

Maybe this is what Joe Biden was talking about back in October when he said if Obama was elected President he would be tested during his first 6 months in office.

A civil war is a pretty big test by most political standards.

Anyhow, Igor – who is apparently channeling a combination of Nostradamus, Chicken Little and Groucho Marx – says that Missouri will be the far southern border of the Central Northern American Republic and will likely be part of Canada.

Illinois and Kansas would also be in the CNAR, but Arkansas would in the Texas Republic along with the entire gulf coast region. They would become part of Mexico.

Kentucky and Tennessee would belong to Atlantic America that would encompass most of the northeast states.

Meanwhile, the western continental US would spin off into the California Republic. Hawaii would become part of China or Japan.

I expect Al-Qaeda to claim the U.S. Virgin Islands.

I don't know about Guam.

Oh, and Russia would take back Alaska. Now, that's a fight I would watch on pay-per-view.

While the Russians would probably take out the Aleutian Islands quickly, the mainland would be another matter. Have they forgotten Afghanistan in the 1980s? Someone should send them a copy of *Charlie Wilson's War.*

I think the general population of Alaska is far better armed and quite a bit crazier than the population of Afghanistan ever was.

Anyhow, I don't think it would be such a bad thing if Missouri became part of Canada.

Canada has reasonable healthcare coverage, back-bacon, SCTV, Michael J. Fox, hockey and those Ice Road Truckers from the Discovery Channel reality show.

I like all of those things.

Missouri already has some Canadian sounding cities. St. Louis, Ste. Genevieve, and Cape Girardeau are all French. Although, we may need to adjust the way we pronounce them to be more Canadian-esque.

Instead of Cape JUH-RAR-DOH, we should probably start saying Cape SHUH-

RAH-DOO. Better start practicing now or you won't fit in. I know I am.

There are some Missouri towns that have names which may not work for Canada and will have to be changed. For instance, Jefferson City may need to be renamed Le Jeffersonville. Poplar Bluff will likely need to be changed to Peuplier Escarpe.

And Jackson will probably have to be rechristened Cape Girardeau Deux.

Sorry, I know having to re-name your town may be traumatic for some people, but we're all going to have to suck it up.

After all, we'll be Canadian. That's what we do.

I really think it will be cool to be the far southern border of Canada. Compared to most of that country, Southeast Missouri would be almost tropical. Think of it. Cape Girardeau could be THE Canadian Riviera. We could be the mecca for Canadian sun-worshiping tourists.

Sure, we don't have an ocean like most rivieras, but we have the Mississippi and you can't spell riviera without a whole lot of help from word "river."

There is one thing about becoming Canadian that I'm not too keen on.

I'm not nuts about having a leaf as my flag.

Not to insult my future country or anything, but can you get a more pansy-ish symbol? Sure, it's a well-designed symbol, but it's still a leaf. Was the ladybug or the dandelion already taken?

I don't understand why Canada did not use something more manly for their flag.

Like a polar bear. They have those.

Or a hockey player. They have those too.

Maybe even an Ice Road Trucker. They definitely have those.

Now, that's a flag other countries would respect.

A Letter From Murray McOinkers

Originally Posted Thursday, April 30, 2009

Dear Humans,

It's bad enough that many of you SOBs like to eat me and my fellow porkers, but I can forgive you for that. I know we are tasty, very tasty.

In fact, just thinking of the McDonald's McRib sandwich gets me all drooly. And let me tell you, crispy thick-cut pepper bacon that practically melts in your mouth is simply to die for.

Occasionally, when I want a midnight snack, but am too lazy to waddle over to the trough, I will nibble on one of my neighbors in the pigpen just to take the edge off. It's usually Phil. He sleeps like a log and never seems to notice. Heck, he doesn't even stop snoring. While, I don't consider myself a cannibal, I must admit we are very, very good eats.

So, I can forgive you for wanting to devour us.

But I can not forgive you for naming a deadly virus after me and my brethren. After all, it was your species' poor hygiene and insatiable ravaging of the Earth's natural resources that stirred up this deadly virus cocktail that is killing your kind. Yet, you have the gall to name it 'Swine Flu.'

That is hogwash!

Don't blame this pandemic on us. The reports we are reading on the Internet indicate that this flu is a mix of swine, avian and human viruses. But do your experts call it Avian Flu or Human Flu or even the Humavine Flu? No, they do not. They call it Swine Flu. Like it is our fault.

Most of us pigs, don't even like the word "swine." That's your word. We find it offensive. It sounds too much like "whine" and while you may hear us squeal once in a while, you will not hear us whine. Most of us are not big complainers.

OK, I'll admit there are a few. I have some cousins who were extras in that movie *Deliverance* with Burt Reynolds and Ned Beatty and they complain all the time about how they were mistreated during the making of the film. But they do have a history of "telling stories" as my mamma used to say, so I take what they tell me with a grain of salt. After all, why would a human do <u>THAT</u> to a pig?

Frankly, I don't think my cousins are all there – if you know what I mean. There's quite a bit of inbreeding over in their neck of the woods, and a lot of my kin – I hate to say this, since they are kin and all, but the truth is the truth – well, they're just not right.

But they are the exceptions. Most of us pigs are just happy to hunker down in the mud and chill out without any whining whatsoever.

I'd like to see any of you humans spend a day in the old hog wallow. Better yet, why don't you tell that Jeff Probst fellow to forget about all those tropical paradises his TV show always goes to and have a season of *Survivor: PigPen.* You humans couldn't survive a week in our muddy mosh pits.

But as I was saying, we don't like the word "swine." It's demeaning, No, we prefer the term "piggy."

And we would prefer you not to name this flu after us and call it for what it actually is, Dirty Human Disease.

Sincerely,
Murray McOinkers

Does A Flashlight Need An 8-Page Manual?

Originally Posted Thursday, January 8, 2009

One of the presents I got for Christmas this year was a flashlight.

It is a Black & Decker Snake Light that uses LEDs rather than traditional bulbs to provide the light. The flashlight has a flexible center section that allows you to bend it into various shapes to make lighting whatever you are looking at easier. It uses two C-batteries and works pretty well.

When I was unpacking the flashlight and installing the batteries, I noticed a warning on the back of the packaging:

"To reduce the risk of injury, user must read and understand instruction manual."

I was a little surprised that a flashlight – even a Snake Light with LEDs – needed an instruction manual.

I was even more surprised that I could somehow injure myself or others with this tool.

After all, it's just a flashlight. How bad could it be?

Perhaps, if I dropped it on my foot and I happened to be shoeless and sockless, then possibly I could give my big toe a bad bruising.

While I often don't read the manuals for the tools that I buy, I felt compelled to read this one, to find out what hazards I could encounter by improperly using my Black & Decker 17 LED Cordless Work Light / Flashlight.

The manual is 8-pages. For a flashlight.

All right, like many product manuals you see these days, half the pages are in Spanish so really the instruction manual is 4-pages.

But still, it's for a flashlight.

So, what critical instructions were included in these 4 pages?

Basically, it detailed all the extreme and very bad things that could occur If I decided to abuse those two C-batteries that came with the flashlight.

For instance, I now know not to take those batteries and throw them in a fire. Something bad would happen, but I don't know what exactly. The manual doesn't say.

What's funny is that I have never – in my entire life – ever considered chucking batteries into a fire. The thought has never ever crossed my mind.

But now that I know something bad could happen if I dropped those batteries into a roaring fire, I feel the urge to do so.

And considering that I have a pile of limbs in my backyard that needs to be disposed of, I actually have a reason to start a fire. But first I need some kindling, something quick to burn that will get that pile ablaze.

What can I possibly use? Wait, I know.

How about an 8-page manual? For a flashlight.

Ralph The Terrorist

Originally Posted Friday, October 16, 2009

I noticed something shocking going to work this past Monday.

The orange traffic cones that have protected the old Federal Building at the corner of Broadway and Fountain were gone! Vanished! MIA! Poof!

THEY WERE JUST NOT THERE!

Now, some people might think that a few missing traffic cones are not a big deal, but I disagree.

These cones have been the only things that have kept the heart of downtown Cape Girardeau safe from terrorists and other nefarious types wishing to make an explosive political statement here in the City of Roses.

I'm not sure exactly when the cones first appeared. It was either after the Oklahoma City bombing or the 9/11 attacks. In either case, the cones showed up and they've been keeping the bad-guys at bay for years. I offer the following evidence as proof that the cones have worked and worked damn well:

Have we had any buildings – Federal or otherwise – blown up in that entire time in Cape Girardeau?

Nope, not a one.

I rest my case.

Now some of you might be thinking, "Why in the world would any terrorist want to even consider attacking the old Federal Building in Cape Girardeau?"

That's a good point and I've thought long and hard about the possible reasons why Cape Girardeau and the old Federal Building could be on some terrorist organization's Things-To-Do list. I concluded there were two viable reasons.

First, Cape is as good of a target as any, maybe even better from a terrorist's perspective. After all, we are in "Podunk, Missouri." We're not expecting to be the target of terrorists so a terrorist would think we were easy pickin's.

Little do they know that the folks of the Heartland have an innate ability to spot anyone who wasn't raised within 30 miles of where they live thus originating that well-known phrase "You ain't from around here are ya... boy?" A spat of chew usually follows this proclamation.

The second reason that Cape and the old Federal Building could be in the terrorists' sights is because of all the dumb terrorists.

Every organization has usually several morons, the idiots who somehow got hired and now thanks to various reasons just can't be let go. Why should a terrorist organization be any different?

For the sake of this discussion, let's call one of these hypothetical idiot terrorists Ralph. I know I could call him Mohamed or Khalid, but that would be stereotyping and stereotyping is bad and never accurate. Nope. Never ever.

Anyhow, Ralph would be the guy who barely squeaked through Terrorist Training

Tech. His professors probably didn't want to have him fumbling around in Bomb Making 101 for another year so they passed him just for showing up to class every day.

But then after graduation, Ralph's handlers would be at a loss as to where to use him. They wouldn't want him involved in the planning of an attack on one of the big cities. He'd probably bungle that operation and get his whole sleeper cell hauled off to GITMO for a little fun-in-the-sun.

No, they would want to save that work for students who graduated magna cum bomba, not the doofus who made it through TTT – *Go Fighting Crusaders!* – out of the sheer grace of his professors and God or Allah or whatever deity was driving his personal train.

So where could they assign him so that he not get caught, but still do some good for their cause?

The Midwest is perfect. If Ralph happened to actually succeed at blowing up something, it would be great PR, a stab in the Heart of the Great Satan. And if not, at least Ralph would be far away from the real terror schemes being cooked up in the big cities.

But, of course, Ralph's plans to blow-up our old Federal Building have long been foiled by a squadron of vigilante orange traffic cones.

I don't know what those cones are made of, but apparently it includes some powerful anti-terrorist juju.

That's why I was so concerned this past Monday, when I drove by the old Federal Building and there was not a cone in sight! Not one!

I don't know if some genius had put them away in deference to last weekend's homecoming parade or what, but as of Monday, our old Federal Building was a sitting duck, defenseless against terrorist attacks.

Thankfully, someone guarding the facility noticed this hole in the perimeter security and took action on Tuesday. The cones were back at their posts once more.

I breathed a sigh of relief when I saw them standing at attention, suspiciously eyeing every vehicle that drove by on Broadway.

The world was safe again.

Ralph the Terrorist had missed his chance.

An Email From Nicole Brown

Originally Posted Wednesday, January 13, 2010

The email arrived at midday and looked urgent. The subject line told me that the sender was "sorry for this unexpected delay."

The sender's name sounded familiar. Nicole Brown. I'd heard that name before. There was the Nicole Brown who OJ Simpson allegedly knifed to pieces back in the 1990s. I was pretty sure the email wasn't coming from <u>that</u> Nicole Brown.

I opened it and read the first paragraph:

How are you doing? I hope all is well with you and your family. I know this might be a surprise to you but I'm writing this email to you in an hurry and in a confused state of mind. I want to say I'm really sorry that I didn't inform you about my traveling to Scotland for a Seminar. It was something urgent and i didn't even inform anyone about this traveling. But I just got myself in serious mess here now. I got my wallet misplaced on my way to the hotel I'm supposed to lodge in. My money,phone, cards,diary, my return ticket and other vital documents are all in the wallet. I'm so confused right now as I have lost all contacts. I can't even book an hotel with the balance on me.

My feelings were a littler hurt after reading that.

Nicole hadn't told me about traveling to Scotland for a Seminar. And it must be a pretty important seminar since she capitalized the word Seminar. Of course, I instantly forgave her for not telling me about her trip, since I seem to have forgotten that I personally knew someone named Nicole Brown. Damn old age. Funny that she could remember my email address, but not my name. I guess we're both getting older.

And what bad luck to have. You take an exciting international trip – an exciting international trip that you fail to mention to practically your best friend, I assume I am her best friend since she did remember my email address – and you misplace your wallet. That sucks.

You know you would think I would have remembered Nicole just from the giant wallet she must have carried around all the time. It had to be huge to carry her money and phone and other vital documents, including her diary. I didn't even know you could fit a diary in a wallet. But then, I'm really not up on ladies fashions.

Or why would you want to carry a diary around with you all the time? I guess it's a habit Nicole picked up pre-Twitter. She probably likes to write down every mundane thing that happens to her in her diary. I sure thought I would have remembered a woman writing in a diary all the time. Maybe I should start drinking ginseng tea. I've heard that it's good for one's memory.

While hindsight is 20/20, I'm really starting to think that Nicole should have invested in one of those wallets that you often see guys wearing that have the giant chain attached to a belt-loop. Short of a pickpocket with bolt cutters, you can't lose one of those wallets. You might even be able to fit a small diary in one of them.

I read on.

I need to get out of this mess. Please I need £2500 to sort myself out here and to pay for the hotel bills but I will appreciate any amount you could afford. I will pay you back as soon as I get back home. Let me know if you will be able to help me with any amount so that i can send you one of my friend over here IBAN account. He can then use his cards to get the moeny for me. But you can send me the money with my details below at any western union money transfer office and i will get the money over here within an hour.

Name : Nicole Brown
Address: 80 High Street, The Royal Mile, EH1 1TH, Edinburgh, United Kingdom
Thank you and look forward to working to hear from you soon
Nicole Brown

I about fell over when I read that Nicole needed 2500 pounds to sort things out and pay for hotel bills. That's about four grand in US dollars. As if I have that much sitting around.

I think Nicole needs to consider staying at a cheaper hotel. Or perhaps she should stay with one of her friends that she so quickly made. It's a guy friend I see from her letter. Typical. I'm pretty sure she always had a lot of male "friends." I wonder why they don't lend her some money?

You know, I think it's about time I un-friend Nicole. She's only there when she wants something from you.

In the meantime, I think I will go to Walgreen's and see if they have some ginko biloba. I remember reading that it might be good for memory. Funny how I can remember something like ginko biloba, but I have no recollection of my friend Nicole. Maybe it will help jog my memory.

Indoor Hunting

Originally Posted Friday, December 19, 2008

I was leaving the grocery store the other evening and noticed a free tourist-type magazine in a rack by the door. The headline on the cover said it was the "Hunting Outdoor Issue."

Which, of course, made me wonder when the Hunting <u>Indoor</u> Issue would be coming out.

I've never been much of a hunter. I wacked a bunny or two growing up with a BB gun, but haven't done much shooting since then except for the occasional pigeon that dared to land on my roof.

I guess if I was a hunter, I would consider myself a fair-weather hunter. If the weather is 70 and sunny and it's sometime after noon, I might consider hunting. But most "hunting seasons" always seem to occur when the weather sucks and you have to get up at 4 in the morning in order to get to your tree stand or hunting blind. That doesn't sound like fun to me.

But I think I could get into hunting indoors.

The weather would always be perfect. And if it did happen to be a little hot or little cool, you could just adjust the thermostat. No rain. No snow. I bet everybody would be hunting indoors.

Locally, Lowe's and Wal-Mart would both be great indoor hunting arenas. First of all, they're both in big buildings. You gotta have space to accommodate all the people who will want to be hunting indoors.

A building like KFC just wouldn't cut it, although that might be a good place to hunt chickens. Free range chickens, of course.

And the buildings have to have tall ceilings, which Lowe's and Wal-Mart definitely do. You're average tree stand would not fit in a Kohl's.

And a big plus for both Lowe's and Wal-Mart is the fact that they already have a small contingent of wildlife living in their stores. Sure, they're just wayward songbirds, but it's a start. After all, prey is prey no matter the size.

Wal-Mart does have one advantage over Lowe's as an indoor hunting arena. If you happen to forget your gun at home, at Wal-Mart you can just head to sporting goods. They'll set you up.

So all Lowe's and Wal-Mart need to do is introduce a little more wildlife to their stores and we'll be ready to go hunting. I was thinking we could start small with a few deer, some turkeys and geese, a family of squirrels and at least one bear to make things interesting.

Then, the Hunting Indoors season could begin.

My plan is almost perfect except for one small thing. As Hunting Indoors takes off - as I'm sure it will - there are bound to be a lot of wayward bullets that will poke holes in the roofs of Lowe's and Wal-Mart. That will let rain in and the heating and air conditioning out. Kind of defeats the whole purpose behind indoor hunting.

To help minimize the roof damage we may need to restrict some guns. No big caliber rifles. No magnums. No Uzis. Nothing bigger than a twenty-two.

And, of course, BB guns would be OK.

I wonder if you can wack a bear with one of those?

"Erosion" A New Concept For Corp of Engineers

Originally Posted Monday, February 2, 2009

I'm no geologist. Most of the geology knowledge I possess came from earth science classes I was required to take back when I was being schooled.

I'm also no engineer although I probably have the technical aptitude to have pursued that profession if I had so desired.

While I am neither of those things, I do think I possess a fair amount of common sense.

That's why I was completely befuddled by an article reporting that some utilities and the U.S. Army Corp of Engineers have spent millions of dollars trying to figure out why parts of the Missouri River are washing away.

This article so dumbfounded me that I actually read it twice while eating my Cheerios that morning.

Perhaps, the "experts" at the Corps of Engineers are not aware of a little concept I learned from my earth science classes long ago.

It's called "erosion."

It usually happens when a liquid – in this case, "water" – washes against another surface – in this case, "the bottom of the river" – causing particles of that surface to break off and float downstream.

If it goes on for several million years, you get a ginormous tourist attraction like the Grand Canyon.

Apparently, what is bothering members of the Corp is the fact that parts of the river bottom are eroding faster than others. In some cases, they've recorded 12 feet of erosion in 50 years. They're afraid that if this continues, it could undermine bridges and levees protecting billions of dollars in development.

Here is another concept the Corp may not be aware of:

The earth is composed of six different types of rock – sedimentary, igneous, metamorphic, gravel, sand and mud. Some of those rocks – sedimentary, gravel, sand and mud – are more susceptible to erosion than the other two. If the bottom of the riverbed has areas composed mainly of those four types of rock, then those areas could erode faster causing parts of the river to be deeper.

Since erosion is apparently a far-fetched explanation of this problem, the Corp is also looking into possible man-made reasons for this predicament.

I guess dredging could be a contributor to this problem. Gee, I wonder what nefarious organization could possibly be doing that on the Missouri River?

I think it's pretty safe to say that fishing is not to blame.

But maybe, the problem is not the fishing, but the fish themselves.

I checked an atlas and found that the Calloway Nuclear Power Plant is about an inch from the Missouri River. It doesn't get much closer than that.

What if, radioactivity from the power plant managed to leak into the river, killing some fish.

And then, what if some catfish – which everyone knows are the garbage-men of the aquatic world – ate some of those dead radioactive fish causing the catfish to grow to monstrous proportions.

Let's say, the size and weight of a Buick from the 1950s.

And since catfish like to live in "honey holes," or pits at the bottom of the river, maybe these Buick-sized nuclear monsters couldn't find any comfortable place in the depths of the Missouri so they just dug out their own "honey holes," thus causing this dilemma that the Corp of Engineers is so concerned about.

This sounds like more of an opportunity rather than a problem to me.

If the word got out that our state had car-sized radioactive catfish lurking at the bottom of the Missouri River, fisherman from all over the world would want to come here to try their luck at reeling one in. They'd stay in hotel rooms. Buy tons of bait. Eat at restaurants. The economic benefits would be phenomenal.

Missouri would have a ginormous tourist attraction.

And, we wouldn't have to wait several million years.

I Are My Own Proof Reader.

Originally Posted Thursday, January 15, 2009

It was pointed out to me the other day that I had misspelled Adolf Hitler's name in not one, but two different blogs. Oops.

I spelled Adolf as Adolph. I should have known better. Those efficient Germans would not waste two letters – "ph" – where a single letter – "f" – would suffice. This illustrates a very important point about my blog.

I are my own proof reader.

Or editor. Or copy editor. Call it what you like, but I'm the only person who reads this blog before it is published on the web. There is no external filter between what I type and what appears on the website.

That's not always a good thing.

An eagle-eyed copy-editor could have pointed out my Hitler faux pas. And they might also point out some of my grammatical errors and run on sentences and question some of my choices for paragraph breaks and the excessive use of the word "anyway" as a transition.

I'll be the first to admit that I am no grammarian. I couldn't diagram a sentence to save my life. Not to be dismissive of English teachers, but I never could see the point in mastering that skill.

However, you will also not see this blog using much of the text messaging slang that is so common with the youth of today. You know, OMG and LOL. I'm not much into using that type of shorthand.

But I do like to link words in a manner that pleases me. As far as my choices of paragraph breaks, I can explain that with one word.

Impact.

Or emphasis would also do. If I want to emphasize a particular sentence, I might make it, its own paragraph, even though it should logically belong to the previous one.

And as far as the use of the word "anyway" as a linguistic transitional device, I find it the most expedient way to get back to the overall point I am trying to make with a given blog.

Sometimes, I get so far off-course that the only way to get back to topic is to write a half-dozen more meandering paragraphs or use the word "anyway."

Anyhow, I tend to write in what I consider a conversational style. While you can and do read these blogs, they could just as easily be read out loud. That's often how I write them, reading them out loud to myself. I think that's why my wife and the cat will often go upstairs to our bedroom to watch TV or read in the evening.

My mumbling drives them crazy.

Thanks four reading.

Incontinent Donuts Need Federal Grant

Originally Posted Monday, February 08, 2010

There are times when I read about some goofy, federal project wasting millions of taxpayer dollar on projects that only benefit a fraction of the population that I think to myself, "Where's my Bridge to Nowhere? Where's my Cash for Clunkers? Where's my Wayfinding Study?"

I feel I pay a lot into The System, but seem to get little in return.

I might sound a little annoyed – actually I'm a lot annoyed – but I would say all is forgiven if the federal government would pony up some dough to conduct research on a serious problem that has been plaguing our country and irritating me personally for years:

Glazed Donut Melt.

Surely, you've witnessed this phenomenon or as it is sometimes called, GDM. When you buy glazed donuts, the icing is always picture-perfect, but after you get them home and they've sat for a while the delicious sugary-coating always seems to start melting away like Vincent Price's face at the end of *House of Wax*. Why is that?

And if you don't catch the melt in time, all you're left with is a semi-sweet and a little chewy donut. And I don't like it.

GDM has perplexed me for most of my adult life. You go to the grocery store in the evening. You pick up a box of tasty looking donuts to have with your coffee the next morning. You leave them nestled snug in their little white box with its little cellophane window and you go to bed.

But then 8 hours later, you wake up ready for donuts and most of the glaze has puddled up in the bottom of the box.

Who wants to eat a bunch of incontinent donuts? I, for one, don't. I buy glazed donuts, because I like the sweet taste of the glaze. If I wanted a naked donut, I'd have a bagel.

And since everybody else seems to be getting a handout from Good Ol' Uncle Sam, I feel my time is due. I want some of my hard earned tax dollars to be spent determining what is causing GDM and how to fix it.

Of course, since I'm so easily fixated by whatever apocalyptic prediction is the current darling of the media, I immediately thought that GDM could be YET ANOTHER sign of global warming.

And if GDM is being caused by global warning, then shouldn't we alert Al Gore so he can look into it?

Oh wait. Scratch that. I just saw a photo of Al.

I could be wrong, but I'm pretty sure he's already been doing extensive field research on this critical issue.

Medical Diagnosis Via Phone App? ¡NOFREAKINWAY!

Originally Posted Wednesday, February 11, 2009

I was watching TV the other night and caught an Apple IPhone commercial promoting the programs or "apps" that are available for the device.

For those of you not familiar with the IPhone, it is designed to allow you to load a variety of software programs developed specifically for the phone. Some of these applications are from Apple, but most come from other vendors. The programs range from useless to useful with likely the vast majority skewing towards the former.

Although, I won't judge since uselessness is really in the eye of the iholder.

Just for the record, I don't have an IPhone. I've played with them. I love the way you can browse the internet with the IPhone, but my work-needs dictate the use of a Blackberry so that is what I carry on my hip. I think there are "apps" available for the Blackberry, but I've never looked into them. I'm happy with email, the occasional web browsing, and the note-taking applications. Oh, and the fact I can make a call as well is a bonus.

But the IPhone has tens of thousands of apps that are designed to make the lives of the IPhone owners a much more bearable existence.

One program called Urbanspoon uses the phone's built in Global Positioning System capabilities to randomly pick nearby restaurants based on simple criteria such as price and food type. You can shake the phone and like a cross between a slot machine and a Magic 8-Ball it will display a nearby restaurant that fits your criteria. If you don't like it, shake the phone again for a new choice.

While most of these apps I could do without, I think this one would be personally nice to have. Sometimes my wife and I have a difficult time deciding where to eat when we go out for dinner. O'Charley's is often our default.

Another app, featured on the TV commercial attracted my attention. It's a program designed to read the medical image files generated by CT, PET and MRI scanners. Those are the very, very expensive scanners used by hospitals to take complex pictures of your innards.

This app troubles me. If I am sick enough that I require an MRI, then I do not – I repeat, <u>do not</u> – want my doctor making a diagnosis based on an image which is 3 inches wide and requires him or her to squint.

"Hmmm Mr. Hollerbach, it looks like you have a tumor. Oh wait, my bad, just a smudge on my IPhone screen. Sorry had some KFC for lunch."

No, if I have to have an MRI, then I'm going to insist that the doctor finds the biggest monitor possible to assist him or her in making the diagnosis. If a stadium Jumbotron is available, that is my preference.

But, if the doctor insists on evaluating me using his $200 toy, then I might be forced to get an IPhone and develop my own app.

UrbanDoc I think I will call it.

Whenever I'm sick, I'll be able to shake my phone, and with any luck it won't stop on an OB/GYN.

Dear Doofuses Sightseeing After The Ice Storm

Tuesday, February 3, 2009

Yes, the ice-covered trees in the park are quite beautiful and worthy of photographs. But perhaps you don't realize how incredibly dangerous these oaks and elms are when they are coated with three-quarters of an inch of ice.

Branches can snap without warning sending hundreds of pounds of wood and ice hurtling to the ground. And if you happen to be under that tree at that time, you will likely be a dead doofus.

I realize that the only people who are likely to be strolling around a park whose trees are ice-covered ticking time bombs are doofuses and junior field reporters for one of the local broadcast TV affiliates.

Normally, if we lost a doofus or two or even a broadcaster to an ice-encrusted falling limb, it would not bother me.

I firmly believe in the concept of "thinning the herd," and if you are stupid enough to take a stroll through a virtual aerial mine field, then you are certainly a worthy candidate for being thinned.

However, I've given that stance a little more consideration and decided that it is in my own selfish interest to warn you that your sightseeing jaunt is a bad idea. You see, with my luck you would be walking under one of those giant oaks when a limb would explode under the weight of the ice and plummet to the ground.

But, rather than killing you – and thus thinning the herd – it would probably just inflict severe head trauma which would leave you an incapacitated vegetable for the rest of your life.

Your family – searching for some way to pay for a nurse to wipe the drool off your chin for the next few decades – would likely sue the city for not personally warning you of the dangers of the park after an ice-storm.

The city's insurance company would settle out of court for some big fat sum, because they know that if your heart-wrenching case went to trial, the jury would probably be made up of a bunch of other doofuses who would award your family even more money

However, insurance companies are businesses, so to pay for the settlement they would jack up the city's liability insurance payments to some astronomical amount. In order to cover the premium, the city would then boost everyone's property taxes including mine.

All thanks to you.

Doofus.

So, please stay out of the park if the trees are ice-covered.

The Death of Buckwheat The Second

Originally Posted Tuesday, March 17, 2009

Our cat's friend died yesterday. Buckwheat the Second was his name.

He'd been dying a fairly slow death, getting more and more yellow with each passing day. You would have thought he had jaundice.

Our cat Patches doesn't have a lot of friends. She might consider the wife and I friends. But more likely she thinks of us as just "The Laps" or "The Keepers of the Purina Cat Chow."

And Smokey – the neighbor's cat – is certainly no friend. Patches despises her with a passion. Smokey is always sneaking into our back yard and Patches doesn't like it one bit. That's Patches' yard. Smokey is definitely no friend.

But Buckwheat The Second was a friend.

Patches would come up from her room in the morning and one of the first things she would do after she got a drink of water, would be to visit Buckwheat The Second. She'd brush her face against him and nibble on him.

Who would have thought that a cat could be friends with a little pot of wheat grass?

But Patches loves grass. When we let Patches out in our backyard to roam she always finds some long piece of grass she can chew on. That's one of the reasons we bought Buckwheat The First at a pet store this past December.

In the winter yard, long pieces of grass are hard to find. And even more so after I mowed the lawn right before Christmas to clean it up.

Back then, Patches was having a hard-time finding a piece of grass in the yard of suitable length that she could chew on.

She actually looked depressed when she would come back in the house from her morning romps outside. Can a cat suffer from S.A.D.?

And so we bought Buckwheat The First and placed his plastic pot on a foam plate next to her feed bowl.

At first Patches didn't know what to make of Buckwheat The First. She knew it was grass, but this grass was inside, not outside. It wasn't right.

But Buckwheat The First was resilient and determined. He was always there sitting by her feed bowl to greet her in the morning. He finally wore Patches down. Patches decided it was OK for grass to be inside. Patches didn't even seem to mind that he had jaundice. Jaundice must be an common ailment with wheat grass.

But Buckwheat The First eventually withered away in January and so, we bought Buckwheat the Second. Patches didn't even seem to notice that a new pot of wheat grass was beside her bowl. She would moosh her face into The Second just as she did into The First.

I fully intended to re-pot Buckwheat The Second – not wanting a repeat ending like we had with his predecessor, but then an ice-storm hit and I got busy and

26 Typos & Awl

yadda, yadda, yadda. That's probably why he died last night.

Actually he likely died last week. He was starting to get that kind of ripe compost odor about him. It was time for him to go.

Will there be a Buckwheat The Third? Maybe, but not until next December. Right now, the grass is greening up and Patches has a yard full of friends.

Thank God for spring.

Haz-Mat Gardening License Optional

Originally Posted Friday, February 27, 2009

A few weeks ago my wife decided that our dining room just wasn't working for us.

We usually have our meals in the kitchen and only once or twice a year would we actually use the dining room for dining. It seemed like a waste of space.

The room – like much of our 95-year-old home – has "decorating challenges" that you might not see in a newer dwelling. Our dining room is not a tidy rectangle, but more of a square with one corner clipped off. There are 4 entryways into the room and it acts as a hallway for much of our home's first floor. The south wall of the room is a large glass bay composed of three windows with an equally large, built-in window seat beneath them.

But my wife – using furniture and various decor we already had on hand – has repurposed the space into our own private coffee-shop-like reading room. It's quite comfortable. It's like being at Starbucks, but without all the laptops.

Last Sunday morning I was enjoying my newspaper and coffee in this room when The Cat decided she needed some lap-time.

Lap-time with The Cat can be 10 minutes or 2 hours or – as it was on this occasion – something in between. I quickly finished reading the newspaper and being one to not sit idle – but also not wanting to disturb The Snoozing Cat – I looked around for something else to occupy my time.

As a part of the room-makeover, my wife has lined up a small collection of vintage gardening books on the window seat – now being used as a giant coffee table – conveniently close to my chair. I could reach these without bothering The Snoozing Cat.

The book I pulled from the collection was *The Complete Book of Garden Magic*. This particular edition was from 1956, but the original printing – and the bulk of the book's content – was from 1936.

I quickly realized that many of the recommended garden solutions from the 1930's would likely require some kind of a haz-mat license in today's world.

For instance, some of the suggested products for fertilizing your lawn back then were "sewer sludge, blood, and tankage."

While it would perhaps not require a hazardous material license, I'm pretty sure my neighbors would not be too thrilled if I spread sewage around my yard, but I bet my grass would look fantastic! And I'm not sure where I would even find enough blood to be effective for my size lawn.

I suppose I could call the Red Cross and check into acquiring their left-over old stock, but they would probably think I was just another a vampire-wannabe rather than a serious gardener.

I had never heard of the term "tankage" prior to reading this book. I looked its definition up and found that it is "the residue from tanks in which carcasses and other offal have been steamed and the fat has been rendered."

I'm guessing it ranks right up there with "sewer sludge" in things your neighbors DON'T want you applying to your lawn.

The book touted arsenate of lead as a great way to kill grubs. And moles could be done in using calcium cyanide powder or peanuts laced with strychnine. I imagine that if you even attempted to acquire any of these substances that someone from the Department of Homeland Security would be paying you a visit.

The book also offered some interesting solutions for taking care of weed problems. It suggested stabbing dandelions with rods dipped in sulphuric or nitric acid. While these may have been easy to acquire in the 1930's, using the latter improperly can result in an explosion according to Wikipedia and the former is regulated by the DEA. Sulphuric acid is used in the manufacturer of meth.

The author also recommended sodium chlorate as a weed killer although he acknowledged it was an "extreme fire hazard." Gasoline was also discussed for this job, but the author "never found it particularly efficient."

But gasoline and kerosene were both endorsed as an effective way of getting rid of ants. Soak their hills, drop a match and run. No suggestion of having a hose handy was offered.

Reading the content from this vintage book actually made me appreciate the fact that a lot of these handy garden "solutions" are not so easily accessible to the general populace any more or they've been packaged in moderation or they have fallen out of favor.

Imagine if soaking an anthill with gas was still the preferred method of eradication:

Well, you know an ounce or two of gas just wouldn't be sufficient. This is America and we love our things "super-sized." If an ounce is good, a gallon must be at least twice or maybe even three times as good.

And if I'm going to all that trouble of blasting out one anthill I might as well take care of the other twenty that are sprinkled throughout my yard.

After a few visits to the gas station – I've got several gas cans, but not enough to hold 20 gallons in one trip – and a thorough dousing of the anthills scattered around my property including one particularly large mound located in the flowerbed beneath our bay window which I gave an extra dousing since it was so gosh-darned big – the only thing left to do would be to light a match and...

...I guess having no bay window could be considered a "decorating challenge."

Health Insurance Form Letter Deserves 'Filing'

Originally Posted Thursday, February 12, 2009

The form letter from Anthem – my wife's health insurance provider – arrived the last week in January.

She said I'd gotten one from them as well the week before, but she had already "filed it." That's our code for chucking it in the trash.

Usually, I would have done the same with this one without more than a cursory glance, but the date stamp caught my eye.

Whenever you get a form letter – especially one regarding insurance or finance – there is usually a date code somewhere on it. Sometimes it might be as subtle as "0209" at the bottom of the page.

But the date stamp on this paperwork was pretty obvious:

"HIPAA Notice 2007" it said on the front page.

The other 3 pages noted that the document was "Effective July 1, 2007."

I immediately wondered why our health insurance company was sending us almost 2-year-old information, just so we could "file it." I read on.

While this form letter came from Anthem, its actual purpose was to tell us all about the HIPAA Privacy Practices. You know, the ones from 2007.

HIPAA is short for Health Insurance Portability and Accountability Act. One of this 1996 law's mandates was to enforce "administrative simplification" in regard to health insurance. I'm not sure how sending out 4-page form letters detailing two-year-old privacy practices is considered "simplification," but then I'm not a bureaucrat.

Perhaps, before the law was enacted, this privacy form letter used one of those fancy script fonts that looked really pretty, but made the document 5 pages long. But now – thanks to HIPAA – they use a nice, no-nonsense serif typeface and use only 4 pages.

Besides being obviously so successful at providing "administrative simplification," the primary purpose of HIPAA is to "enhance health insurance accessibility for people changing employers or leaving the workforce."

As far as my wife and I are concerned, we're neither planning on changing employers or quitting our jobs. I've been with the newspaper for 16 years and my wife is a tenured associate professor at the local university.

Do the HIPAA bureaucrats know something we don't?

I guess you never know with the sorry state of the economy. Maybe I wrote one too many smart-aleck blogs about the university, and its higher-ups have decided to teach me a lesson via my wife. I did mention she was tenured, didn't I?

Being tenured faculty doesn't make you "bullet-proof" from downsizing, just really, really "bullet-resistant."

Perhaps, the government bureaucracy that administers HIPAA is instructing all of the health insurance companies to send out this paperwork based on some federal study that indicates we are ALL likely going to lose our jobs and this way we will be prepared to be portable with our insurance.

I'm not sure where we will all work if that does happen, but thanks to HIPAA our privacy will be protected.

So don't be surprised if you, your spouse, your kids and your pets each get one of these 4-page form letters.

As for me, I'm not counting on my job sticking around so I've started sending out resumes. Topping my list is a position with the city Public Works department.

I've got a hunch they will be needing more trash men.

After all, someone has to take care of this increase in "filing."

How to Write a Blog In FOUR EASY STEPS!

Originally Posted Monday, September 14, 2009

My co-worker Chris is scheduled to teach a class for the local university's Extended and Continuing Education program on blog writing. She is going to teach four ninety-minute classes over a four-week period starting October 29.

Personally, I think she has her work cut out for her.

If I taught the class, it would likely wind up meeting one time and lasting about 2 minutes. Here are the four steps I apply to almost every blog I write:

1. Find something that interests me.
2. Start writing.
3. Stop when I think I am done.
4. Revise as necessary.

That's the whole class if I were to teach it. I'd give my two minutes of sage advice then ask my students if anyone wanted to go get a beer. Since I've written a blog or two that involved beer I think that would be OK. We could consider it field research on blogging.

Granted, I probably don't write what would be considered a "traditional" blog. A lot of blogs are journals documenting the blogger's daily life. Essentially they are online diaries. However, I don't believe the *SEMissourian.com* has many bloggers like that. It has more bloggers who specialize in posting about a particular area of interest or expertise.

Since, I am interested in many things and claim expertise in absolutely nothing, I tend to write about whatever attracts my attention. In many ways I'm a lot like the dog in the animated movie *Up* who is constantly distracted by wildlife.

SQUIRREL!

OK, I know I said my blog lecture would be only about 2 minutes long. Well, that was the Reader's Digest version. Basically, I cut out all the fluff in my two-minute version.

Usually, when I actually write a blog, I leave all the fluff in. Sometimes there's so much fluff that you can't even tell what the point of a particular blog actually was. Sometimes, I don't even know. Didn't someone once say, that sometimes the journey is more important than the destination?

Anyhow, for the sake of filling space, let's go over my...

...PATENTED four-step blog writing process that can be ALL YOURS for the LOW, LOW PRICE of only $19.95 plus shipping and handling. BUT WAIT! THERE'S MORE! If you order RIGHT NOW we'll throw in our FREE GUIDE showing you how to name your blog – a FIFTY DOLLAR VALUE – absolutely FREE if you order WITHIN THE NEXT TEN MINUTES! Operators are standing by so DON'T DELAY!

Sorry, about that. I occasionally find myself possessed by the spirit of recently deceased pitchman Billy Mayes. It's kind of annoying.

So let's look a little closer at my four-step process. Before you write a blog, you need to find something that interests you to write about. It can be anything. I tend to be fascinated by the minutiae of life that often gets overlooked.

Oh sure, I could write about BIG PICTURE issues like Obama's healthcare reform initiative, but that requires a lot of work. Do I really want to read a thousand-page document that is only a draft? Nope.

And I think too many bloggers tend to base their opinions on the opinions and summations created by others rather than reviewing the original source material on a given issue. If I'm going to write about something, I prefer to use my own interpretative lens.

After you come up with your idea, the next step is to start writing. When I start a blog, I rarely have any idea how it will end. Sometimes I *never* figure out how a given blog will end. That might explain why I currently have approximately 150 blogs in various stages of development filed on my laptop. Starting is one of the top three hardest things about writing a blog. The other two are stopping and putting the stuff in between.

My goal in starting a blog is to make it grab attention. Is paragraph one interesting enough that a reader will want to read paragraph two and so on and so forth?

After getting started I just keep writing. Sometimes I attempt to cover an entire topic, but that is rare. Often I will write at least 500 words and then start thinking of braking. As I said, stopping is the second hardest thing about blog writing. Since most of my blogs are intended to be more humorous in nature – they make me laugh anyway – I like to end on a chuckle if I can.

Some bloggers like to question their readers, and will ask them what they think about a particular issue. The way I look at it, you don't have to ask the readers for feedback. If they have an opinion, they will give it to you whether you want it or not.

The stuff between starting and stopping is sometimes challenging to write. I find that if you have a good start, the middle just writes itself. Of course, it helps that many of my blogs are not what you call "research intensive." Personally, I don't want to work that hard. I write these things to amuse me as much as anything.

The last step of my PATENTED blog writing process is to REVISE, REVISE, REVISE! YOU TOO can revise your own blogs in JUST FIVE EASY STEPS. Learn how to edit your own BLOGS that can be PUBLISHED on the INTERNET where they can be SEEN by MILLIONS OF PEOPLE.

If you call RIGHT NOW we'll send you our PATENTED four-step blog writing process, your FREE GUIDE on how to name your blog – a FIFTY DOLLAR VALUE – AND our guide to revising your own blogs in JUST FIVE EASY STEPS ALL for only $29.95 plus shipping and handling. Operators are standing by. CALL NOW!

I'm so sorry. I'm really not sure why the ghost of pitchman Billy Mayes is

haunting me. If this keeps up I may have to look into an exorcism.
    SQUIRREL!

Sheep Burping Research

Originally Posted Monday, March 2, 2009

While I don't closely follow the research being conducted on livestock flatulence, I have heard that it – or more specifically, the methane emitted by farting cows – is a significant contributor to global warming.

Whether it is or isn't, is anyone's guess. For the sake of this discussion, we will consider it a legitimate problem.

Now the little amount of information I have absorbed about this topic made me believe that cow farts were a major conspirator in this crime against the climate.

But apparently gassy Guernsey's are not the leading contributors of livestock methane in the atmosphere.

It's actually venting from the other end that is the problem. Yes, I'm talking bovine belches.

According to an article in last Thursday's *Wall Street Journal*, intensive research on livestock emissions is being conducted in New Zealand. They have what is described as the world's foremost research facility on the study of livestock farts and burps.

They're doing this for a couple reasons.

First of all, they're concerned that due to the increased awareness of global warming, international rules could be created which require countries to control the emissions of their livestock.

And secondly, New Zealand has a heckuva lot of livestock.

They have millions of cows and goats, but the focus of their emissions research is on sheep, and for good reason. The country has an estimated 35 million of them. That's 10 for every person living in New Zealand. I can only imagine what would happen to the polar ice caps, if all those sheep farted at the exact same time. I wonder if Al Gore has looked into this situation?

Even if he hasn't, a number of scientists down in New Zealand are busy studying the issue – the over-all problem of livestock methane emissions that is, NOT what would happen if all their sheep farted simultaneously.

And in all honesty, the study of Unison Flock Flatulating is really more of a fringe science in the world of livestock digestive research. The odds of a U.F.F. event sizable enough to cause immediate and catastrophic climatic change are pretty slim.

While U.F.Fs may not be considered a threat, the over-all amount of gas being vented by livestock is being taken quite serious in New Zealand.

Using special "respiration chambers" their scientists have been able to measure the amounts of methane the sheep are emitting. They've found that while livestock – this includes sheep and cows – produce some methane when farting, significantly more is released by way of belching.

Humans also emit methane, but reputedly in much lower quantities. I say reputedly since I personally have yet to see if there is any current research on this subject.

Maybe all of the exploration that has been conducted on human methane emissions was actually done in the 1950s, years before the proliferation of buffalo wings and Bud Light. You can't tell me, that combination doesn't produce some serious amounts of methane.

But I digress.

While studying the burping sheep, the scientists in New Zealand have been attempting to lessen the amount of methane the livestock emit by varying the diet of the test animals. So far this has not yielded any worthwhile results.

I personally think this sheep burping research is headed in a baaaad direction. Rather than trying to minimize the burping, perhaps we should be encouraging the livestock to belch even more.

What if rather than trying to control the emissions, we worked at creating a way to harness the raw power of all this livestock gas using some kind of device that could capture and contain that precious methane? It could then be collected and used for the good of mankind.

Imagine if we all had a few sheep in our backyards, each of them hooked up to one of these emissions collections devices – we'll call it a bleat-exchanger. Whenever you need to go somewhere in your methane-powered car, you just go out to your personal flock, and fill 'er up.

And as a bonus, if some unexpected guests showed up for dinner, you have rack of lamb ready and waiting on the hoof.

Now, that's an alternative energy source I can believe in.

Dear Doofus In The White Buick At The ATM

Tuesday, February 10, 2009

It's been 5 minutes, and the two cars ahead of me and the three cars behind me have not moved an inch. I knew it was a bad sign, when you pulled up to the drive-thru ATM and proceeded to get out of your car.

You then fed several pieces of paper into the machine. I guess these were checks. The ATM then printed out receipts that you studied as if you were prepping for a physics test.

Meanwhile another car pulled in behind me.

I can't imagine what is taking you so long, but I will give you a bit of financial advice that you may not realize. Just because you have checks in your checkbook, does not mean you still have money in your account.

You appear to be someone who may not have realized that fact.

Another car has pulled into line. We are now up to 8, counting your Buick. Good thing Bank of America has a big parking lot.

Now, you are scratching your head. You look at the machine as if it is a Martian and slowly get back into your car. Joy! You appear to be getting ready to leave. But then a lady gets out of the passenger side of your car and walks around to the ATM. Thankfully she puts no checks in the machine.

A Nissan at the back pulls out of line. The car drives slowly by your Buick, honks and its driver – a guy, of course – salutes you with both middle fingers raised proud. He then screeches off down William Street presumably in search of another ATM. You seem oblivious to either the salute or to the traffic jam you are creating. Two more cars replace the Nissan.

Meanwhile, the woman has been putting in cards and punching in pin numbers and studying receipts that the ATM spits back at her. I've not seen any money actually come out.

I'm starting to wonder if you and your companion are attempting to refinance your mortgage. That's the only explanation I can think of for taking this long at an ATM. Two cars behind me have pulled out of line. I would do the same, but I'm boxed in and can only go forward.

The woman finally finishes and walks back around to the passenger side of your Buick. She gets in and you slowly pull off.

I hope I never see you again.

'Old School' Heating

Originally Posted Friday, March 05, 2010

The school district in Perry County, Missouri has been awarded almost one million dollars in stimulus grant money to switch to a wood-burning heating system.

The computer-controlled system will manage both a conveyor that will automatically feed wood into the furnace and fans that will control how fast it burns, according to an article in the *Southeast Missourian*.

Apparently, the district is going "old school" with its building heating, although I personally don't think it is "old school" *enough*. While the fuel might be "old school," the system itself is definitely "new school" and at the price, I don't like it.

Now some people might wonder why I should even care how Perry County heats their public school since I don't live there or have ever lived there. They'd be right. I am not an immediate stakeholder in anything to do with that county, but I care because that stimulus grant money is tax money, and therefore it is my money.

While I think it is a fantastic idea that they heat their school with wood, what's wrong with good old potbelly stoves? Do you know how many potbelly stoves the Perry County School District could buy with the $970,000 grant they're getting from the Missouri Department of Conservation?

1700.

And we're not talking about just any old generic potbelly stove, but a Vogelzang 200,000 BTU Potbelly Stove direct from Amazon.com and that includes shipping.

I could be wrong, but I'm pretty sure that the Perry County School District doesn't have 1700 classrooms to heat so I bet that they would only need to spend perhaps a tenth of the grant money to buy and install a potbelly in every classroom rather than getting this high-tech computerized gizmo.

With a potbelly stove, there aren't a lot of parts that can break, just a couple of doors and a couple of dampers to adjust airflow. That's it. Even a first-grader can troubleshoot the problems on a potbelly stove. They don't need to go to some fancy-schmancy HVAC training course to find out how to program a computer and which sensors can stop the whole system dead in its tracks if they malfunction.

With a potbelly in every classroom the Perry County public school system could expect decades of low cost heating with very little maintenance. Just clean the flues once a year and take out the ashes daily. That's it.

And on top of that, students would learn valuable life lessons like touching an active potbelly stove in the winter will cause a nasty burn, and how to cut kindling with a hatchet, and the best way to properly stack a cord of wood. For those who are curious, you turn every other layer 90 degrees to the one below it at the ends of the stack.

As an added bonus, rather than sending unruly children to the principal's office or detention, teachers could have them work off their indiscretions the old fashioned way with a sledge and wedges.

"Billy, I saw you throw that spit wad at Sarah. Out to the woodpile! I want to see a split cord of oak by the end of the day, mister, and it better be stacked properly when you are done."

HCR 99 – Saluting the Reese's Peanut Butter Egg

Originally Posted Friday, March 6, 2009

I think I know why I have never aspired to be a politician.

First of all, I try to be concise. Sure, I will ramble on and I have been known to use colorful language for the sake of the color, but it doesn't compare to the long-windedness that a lot of politicians are masters of.

And secondly, I like periods. You know, periods. Those little dots at the end of sentences.

The opposite of both of these characteristics can be found in House Concurrent Resolution 16 – or HCR 16 as it is also known – that just passed the Missouri House of Representatives this week by a vote of 125 to 29.

Let me summarize this resolution for you:

Missouri does not want any of the suspected terrorists from the Guantanamo Bay prison either detained here or transported through our state and we encourage the eight states that share our borders to adopt a similar resolution.

There you go. That's the whole resolution. However, I used 37 words rather than the 419 that actually compose HCR 16, not including the title.

Perhaps, the legislator who introduced it started with my appropriately concise version, but then realized that 37 words would look pretty pathetic printed a sheet of paper.

So rather than using 48-point type to make the 37 words cover an entire page, he decided to flesh it out a bit more by adding a "Whereas" here and a "Now, therefore" there and a whole lot of other details that everyone already knows, until he got to the 419 words which comprise HCR 16, not including the title.

The one thing that my 37-word version has in common with the official 419-word version is the same quantity of punctuation. We both used one period. You know, those little dots at the end of sentences.

Now, don't get me wrong because I'm not picking on this particular legislator or legislation. All official Resolutions like this one appear to follow some historical and/or legal precedents that treat punctuation as unnecessary and consider long-windedness a virtue. Thankfully, a lot of Bills are not written this way.

Now you might be saying to yourself, "Brad, what exactly is the difference between a Bill and a Resolution?"

I'm glad you asked, because I was wondering the exact same thing, so I looked it up.

Bills are how a law is made. After a Bill passes both houses of the legislature and is signed by the governor, it is then an enforceable law.

In comparison, Resolutions are meant to either make a statement or to honor a person, organization, event or issue. Their purpose is to make various people look or feel better.

Legally-speaking, resolutions are meaningless.

I looked at some of the other Resolutions that have been proposed in the Missouri House this year and they include one that encourages MODOT to install a stoplight at a particular intersection in Weldon Springs (HCR 1) and another that urges dogs to be "Canine Good Citizens" (HCR 4).

After reading about the attempt to legislate the behavior of dogs, I realized that anyone can write a Resolution about practically anything so I thought I would give it a try.

Since, Easter is fast approaching and a lot of people – myself included – really like the Reese's Peanut Butter Eggs, I think the Missouri Legislature should consider a resolution honoring that candy. We will call it HCR 99:

Whereas, the H.B. Reese Candy Company, a division of The Hershey Company makes several special Holiday versions of their peanut butter and chocolate confection and

Whereas, it is known to this body that these Holidays include Halloween, Christmas, Valentine's Day and Easter and

Whereas, these confections come in various shapes pertinent to their given Holiday and

Whereas, it is agreed upon that all of these confections are quite tasty, but that one of the four known Holiday versions of the Reese's peanut butter and chocolate candy is tastier than the others and

Whereas, the reason decided upon was that that particular Holiday confection appears to the Legislature to have more of the sweet peanut butter filling than contained in the others:

Now, therefore, be it resolved that the members of the House of Representatives of the Ninety-fifth General Assembly, First Regular Session, the Senate concurring therein, that the Reese's Easter Holiday Confection is the best tasting of the four known Holiday versions of this historic candy and

Be it further resolved that this body, declares the Reese's Peanut Butter Egg the official Spring Sweet for the State of Missouri.

I would say my resolution is just about perfect.

It has several "Whereases" and a "Now, therefore," and lots of other details that most people are probably already aware of.

I even made sure to use just one period. You know, those little dots at the end of sentences.

I Don't Get 'The Rich'

Originally Posted Monday, March 08, 2010

I don't get the rich.

I'm not rich, never have been rich and probably will never be rich so perhaps that's why I don't get the rich.

They sometimes do things that completely baffle us non-rich people.

For instance, I recently read in the *Wall Street Journal* about how the popularity of oil paintings of former Federal Reserve chief Alan Greenspan has waned.

At that point, I was already scratching my head.

Unless you also knew Mr. Greenspan as "dad" or "pa-pa" or were closely related in some other way, why on earth would anyone want to have a picture of him, much less an oil painting?

I realize that art is in the eye of the beholder. I own a couple of signed prints by artist James Bama who specializes in highly detailed portraits of cowboys, Indians and mountain men. His level of detail is amazing, almost photographic. I like his work, but I own prints, not original oil paintings and the most expensive one cost about a hundred bucks.

In comparison, this article profiled people – presumably rich people – who spent thousands of dollars for portraits of Greenspan that they could hang in their offices or their homes. Some were paintings and some were limited edition prints. One guy from Tampa Bay paid $150,400 for a painting of the fed chief at an online auction in 2006.

But now the paintings and prints and the former fed chief have lost their luster. Some of the rich people who acquired the artwork have even put theirs into storage. The guy from Tampa says he keeps his under his bed.

What a massive waste of money. I don't know about you, but if I'm going to own a painting of the former fed chief then my last name had better be Greenspan and the last time I checked, it wasn't.

I have a lot better things to do with my money such as buying scratch-off lottery tickets.

I've heard that's one sure fire way to get rich.

This Blog Is For The Birds

Originally Posted Monday, April 12, 2010

Our cat Patches likes routine. She has little rituals that she follows and expects The Laps – that's my wife and I – to follow. Frankly, she's like a little general.

One of these routines is that every morning when we let her out of her room in the basement – actually it is more of a kitty condo complete with endless buffet, various places to snooze and a nice view of the outdoors – she wants her tour of the backyard before she comes back in for breakfast consisting of Purina Cat Chow.

Patches' primary points of interest in our yard are the two bird feeders that attract a variety of birds and the highly-determined squirrels who live in our elm trees. Since we don't particular want Patches' catching a bird or tackling with a squirrel, when she goes out, so do I.

I make my rounds to verify that no wildlife is foraging on the ground beneath the feeders and if they are there, to shoo them away.

Really, the only reason I feel compelled to be a backyard foot soldier for General Patches is because of the several mourning doves that like to congregate in our backyard for the feed.

Mourning doves are fat birds, and because of their weight they couldn't eat at our squirrel-resistant bird feeders even if they wanted to. A door closes over the feeding trough if too much weight – such as an obese mourning dove or a scavenging squirrel – tries to sit on it.

But the mourning doves don't appear to mind. They seem quite happy to waddle around beneath the feeders scrounging up bits of black-oil sunflower seeds that have been dropped or raked out of the feeders by some other bird.

I've observed these birds for many years and I've noticed something about mourning doves.

They are the Forrest Gump of the bird community. They are oblivious to almost everything until the very last second.

"Momma always said life is like a feeder full of black-oil sunflower seeds. You never know what might fall to the ground."

I'm not really sure what General Patches would exactly do if she ever caught one of the mourning doves. She would probably try to lug it up to the porch like she did with a songbird last summer. Of course, the songbird was an eighth of the size of the mourning doves.

That bird got lucky and managed to escape when I picked up Patches.

It helps that the General is ticklish.

Burglar-Proofing Your Home With Bert And Ernie

Originally Posted Monday, March 9, 2009

I was discussing the rash of break-ins that have been occurring throughout the city with my friends Bert and Ernie.

Bert is convinced that his neighbors are behind the crime spree.

"Look," he said pointing to the map I created for a previous blog that plotted all the reported break-ins since January 1.

"There aren't any break-ins in the middle of the city and look who is in the dead center, where not one robbery has occurred: <u>my neighbors</u>."

Bert is suspicious that the people next door to him are stealing jewelry from homes around town and refining it into gold bars.

"Why else would they have some of their windows open all the time even when it is 10 degrees outside!"

Ernie chimed in. "Bert they're not refining gold. They're making meth."

"Well, of course they're making meth! They're doing that in the backroom and smelting the gold into ingots in the basement," Bert countered. "Who knows what other nefarious criminal enterprises are happening in that house. Counterfeiting. Identity-thieving. Telemarketing. It wouldn't surprise me if they were hosting one of them al-Qaeda sleeper cells in their garage."

Ernie's advice to both of us was to get an alarm system. He was getting one to put his wife at ease.

"How much does a camera system cost?" Bert asked me. "If one of these SOBs breaks into my house, I want to get a picture of them that I can hand over to the cops."

That's a pretty worthwhile strategy. Then Bert just needs to lure the thieves to his house so they can be photographed. That might be pretty easy if they are indeed living next door.

I guess Bert can take a cue from some of those deer hunting shows they're always airing on the Outdoor Channel. Maybe he can hang some jewelry and dollar bills from the trees in his front yard and spray his bushes with cologne that would attract felons – buck scent or burga-lure, perhaps – to let these thieves know his house was ripe for robbery.

And then, of course, hope they don't steal his camera system while they are pilfering his stuff.

Personally, I'm covering all my bases. Besides installing alarm and camera systems, I'm planning on renting a backhoe this weekend and putting in my own moat that I'm going to stock with a school of piranha. One or two of those fish just wouldn't do. You have to have at least a couple hundred for impact.

And then, I'm going to replace my 6-foot tall wooden privacy fence with a 10-foot tall brick wall with a few strategically placed guard towers complete with gun-turrets. On top of my wall, I'm going to add a nice layer of broken glass with a few strands of barbed wire.

Yes, I know my wall – but not the moat – will violate local zoning codes, but desperate times call for desperate measures. I figure if the city can't protect my property, then why should I pay attention to their rules pertaining to my property.

Besides, I feel like I'm doing my part to stimulate the economy.

Backhoe rental is not cheap and the bricks-and-mortar-laying and barb-wire-stretching businesses don't work for free.

And have you checked into how much an entire school of piranha costs? It's expensive. Not to mention the cost of their upkeep. Just one bag of Purina Piranha Chow is outrageous.

But when it is all done I will be able to sleep more soundly at night knowing that even if a burglar made it over my brick wall and didn't cut himself to shreds on the glass and barb wire and then somehow got across my piranha-filled moat without being chewed to pieces and actually did manage to break into my house without setting off my security systems, that there will be nothing left for him to steal.

I would have already pawned it all to pay for my piece of mind.

Economic Impact BULLSHEET

Originally Posted Monday, October 05, 2009

I've always been suspicious of "economic impact" claims made by governments and institutions. They invariably appear to be outrageously high with little supporting evidence to back them up.

Of course, the governments and institutions never directly make those assertions. They always outsource the research to third-party companies to give the claims a sense of independent validity that we of the rank and file are supposed to take as the gospel.

One of these recent "economic impact" claims was released last Thursday regarding the 2009 Tour of Missouri bicycle race. The report by German-based consulting firm IFM Sports concluded that people attending the 2009 Tour of Missouri bicycling race spent over $38 million.

I immediately wondered if they had a decimal out of place. $3.8 million sounded more like it to me. But then the article noted that spending was up over $8 million from the 2008 Tour of Missouri race.

Could the "economic impact" experts who did this analysis for the state of Missouri have gotten the decimal point wrong TWO years in a row? It sounded incredulous, but no more so than this cycling event having actually generated $38 million of "economic impact" for our state.

This extraordinary claim got me thinking.

What exactly is the economic impact of this blog?

After extensive analysis, I have calculated that the annual economic impact of *The Irony Of It All* essays is about $11,128,026.

Now, if you think I just pulled that number out of thin air, you are wrong. In fact, after conducting a thorough survey of several of my co-workers, I took those results along with other research and extrapolated them through a highly complex economic algorithm that I personally designed which I call Brad's Unequaled Levelheadedly-Legitimate Strategically-Honest Economically-Ethical Theorem or BULLSHEET, for short.

Before delving into the intricacies of BULLSHEET, I thought I might share some of the responses from my co-workers that are not really relevant to the economic impact analysis of my blog, but I felt were still interesting.

Two of my co-workers read my blog "occasionally."

One reads it "when it looks like it might be funny."

Another never reads my blog and never will because we mutually think the other is an idiot.

Three did not realize I wrote a blog for our website.

One did not realize the *Southeast Missourian* had a website.

OK, so surveying my co-workers may not be the most highly scientific method in the world, but I believe it's a start and has about as much validity as anything done by firms who specialize in calculating "economic impacts."

Now, I can't divulge all the inner workings of BULLSHEET – it's highly proprietary and that makes it very valuable – but I can share some information explaining how I determined that this blog has a $11,128,026 economic impact on our economy.

For starters, it is viewed an average of 6500 times a month. Now according to the BULLSHEET formula, I estimate that more than one person – 2.29 people to be exact – is viewing these pages at a time. This takes into account the 1.3 people who are looking over your shoulder while you are reading – Trust me, they are there – which works out to 14,885 persons perusing this blog each month.

Since I tend to be a bit wordy, I figure that each of these essays takes the average person an average of 15 minutes to read.

Now, based on our website log data, most of this reading – 89% to be exact – takes place from workplaces. Therefore, if the average hourly rate plus benefits of the typical workplace reader is a conservative $40, collectively these readers are frittering away $132,476.50 of their employers' compensation goofing off each month reading these essays.

OK, while that doesn't sound very positive, it is still impacting the economy, just not in a way that most people would define as "good." But the way I look at it, impact is impact, good or bad.

And you should also know that sometimes a multiplier might be used in "economic impact" research that takes into account the fact that every dollar spent turns over several times generating even more economic impact.

Even though I've shown you that this blog is responsible for over $132,000 in lost employee productivity each month, I don't see why this multiplier can't be used.

After all, every time a reader goofs off at work and reads one of these rants, isn't it likely that either they have to work overtime or that someone else has to pick up the slack? And then someone else has to do that person's work and so on and so forth. It makes perfect sense to me.

That's why the multiplier in my formula is seven, which means that this blog generates $927,335.50 in economic impact each month or $11,128,026 a year.

I think it's pretty irrefutable. After all, you can't dispute BULLSHEET.

Magazine 'Free Gift' Leaves Something To Be Desired

Originally Posted Monday, March 15, 2010

I'm trying to reform myself when it comes to dealing with mail. And by mail, I mean the old-fashioned kind that gets delivered to your house 6-days-a-week rather than the type that shows up on your computer 24/7.

My wife and I have a tray on our home's built-in butler's pantry that we've designated for all new old-fashioned mail.

Our original goal was that new mail would only stay there briefly before being moved to the bill organizer, put into the filing file folder, shredded or pitched.

Unfortunately, that's not how it has worked out.

The mail has been getting put in the tray, but then we don't deal with it right away, so the stack gets higher and higher until we have an incident like we had last week. The pile toppled over covering our cat who was strolling by in credit card check offers, bills and spring gardening catalogs.

It rather traumatized her. Rather than sauntering by the pantry like she's done for years she now gallops past it, obviously afraid that she's going to be beaned again in the head by a *Plow & Hearth* catalog.

Ever since the mailanche, I've been trying to be better at dealing promptly with the mail. So last Friday I was reviewing that day's pile when I came upon an envelope that I would normally toss without a second glance.

It was a magazine offer from *Fortune* magazine. The envelope said "Do Not Bend." I thought that was curious for a magazine offer, so I opened it up. The reason the envelope said *"Do Not Bend"* was because it contained a free gift enticing me to subscribe to *Fortune.*

It was a bookmark.

With an imposing name like *Fortune,* you'd practically expect the free bookmark to be made of gold just to show me that if I truly wanted to make a fortune that *Fortune* magazine is the-end-all-be-all, absolute only source that wannabe fortune pursuers should turn to for advice on how to both make and spend a fortune and that because Time, Inc. – the publishers of *Fortune* – had sent me a gold bookmark that I would be completely daft not to subscribe to their magazine. At least, that's what I expected.

But sadly, the bookmark was not made of gold or any metal for that matter. It was not even made of plastic. No, this bookmark was made of cardboard and when I say it was made of cardboard, it was actually about the thinnest piece of cardboard they make. It was kind of like heavily starched typing paper.

It was rather disappointing. I could use some good fortune right now. Do you have any idea how much a pet psychiatrist costs for a cat who has been traumatized by mailanche?

Logging Reality Shows Have Room For One More

Originally Posted Wednesday, April 07, 2010

I'm addicted to TV shows about loggers.

I'm not really sure why. Perhaps it's the outdoorsy aspect of the shows or the sense of danger. Logging is the second deadliest occupation in the US behind being a commercial fisherman.

I did some logging growing up, but nothing on the scope or scale of the reality shows they air on TV. Really, about the only things these TV shows and my teenage logging experiences have in common are chainsaws. Well, that and trees. You can't be a logger without trees, can you?

No, we didn't have massive pieces of equipment that allow today's professional loggers to efficiently harvest trees from incredibly steep terrain or monstrous machines that can cut the limbs off of a fallen tree and slice it into trailer-sized length in mere seconds.

We just had dad's McCullough chainsaw, an old International Harvester tractor, a wagon that had been put together using the back half of an old pickup truck, our own muscle and the 84-acre property owned by my parents that was half-covered by woods. That was it.

Really, our logging experiences wouldn't have made much of a TV show. It would have been pretty lame, except for maybe that one time when the parking brake on the tractor slipped and it started rolling downhill without a driver.

I never saw my dad ever move faster than that moment.

But I enjoy following the load competitions on The History Channel's *Ax Men* and the totally alien world of *Swamp Loggers* on Discovery and the family of Maine woodsmen on *American Logger.* While the logging reality-show market may appear to be at capacity, the other weekend I was in my backyard and realized there might be room for just one more.

My 100-year-old backyard elm trees had not yet leafed out and I could easily see a few broken limbs, presumably remnants from the big ice storms of last year.

While contemplating these dangling branches, one of the squirrels that live in my backyard jumped from the canopy of our one big elm to the canopy of the other. That's when I had the idea for my logging reality show:

American Squirrel Tree Trimmers

Squirrels are already tree-trimmers in their own right. Squirrels build tree nests out of short limbs they've chewed from the tree. Whenever a windstorm comes along and blows one nest away, the squirrels just build another.

Wild squirrels just use limbs and twigs that they've randomly chosen. But what if we could train them to be better arborist, to sculpt the trees to our liking?

And then what if we could get them to wear little hardhats and tiny flannel shirts and train them on how to use just-their-size miniature chainsaws that they could wield against limbs a little too big for them to chew through?

And since all good reality shows need some dramatic tension, what if we made sure to have some young "greenhorn" squirrel tree trimmers who are constantly screwing up.

Or maybe we could include a crazy rabid squirrel logger who would do the unexpected. Or perhaps we could even get a team of beavers to give the show some competitive tension. Squirrel loggers versus beaver loggers. I like that.

I think that would be a show people would want to watch.

And if the *History* or *Discovery Channels* weren't interested, there's always *Animal Planet*.

Dear Doofus in the Camaro on Route K

Originally Posted Wednesday, April 08, 2009

I bet you flunked coloring in kindergarten. I wasn't so hot about staying in the lines myself, but then I grew up and I got better at it. Apparently, you did not.

And because you appear to have failed coloring in kindergarten, you may not realize that the highway department paints those lines on the roadway for reason.

Now, before I go any further, I want to make sure you are paying attention. You're not talking on your cell phone, applying eyeliner and eating a breakfast burrito while attempting to drive, as you were this morning, right?

I know you might think you're a "multi-tasker," but let me be the first to tell you that you are not. While I don't know you personally, I think it is a safe to say that you may barely qualify as a "uni-tasker."

It's OK. It's not your fault. People get a lot of their tasking abilities from their parents, so if you are not able to do more than one simple task at a time, it's their fault, not yours. You should tell them the next time you see them that your shortcomings are all because of them.

And if that next time happens to be this Easter Sunday, I guarantee it will make for a very spirited holiday gathering that no one in your family will soon forget.

Besides letting your parents know about flaws their genetics have inflicted on you and considering the number of things you were attempting to get done while driving, I might also suggest that you take a small portion of your next paycheck – about $10 – and buy yourself a new alarm clock. Apparently, the one you are currently using is not working properly if you are forced to attempt so many personal maintenance projects while also driving.

But I digress. We were discussing the lines on the road.

First of all, there are the yellow lines you see in the middle of the road. You seem to know that crossing them is bad. That is good. Crossing yellow lines can result in things like a head-on collision. That is NOT how you want to start your morning. It could result in your eyeliner getting smudged and you wouldn't want that to happen.

But you seem to have a problem with the dashed white lines. They are meant to divide two lanes of traffic. One lane of traffic drives on the right side of the line while the other drives on the left. Under no circumstances should you drive down the middle of the white line as you were doing this morning. The dashed white line is not a coupon and your Camaro is not a pair of scissors.

You need to be decisive and pick a side – either right or left. Driving down the center is not an option.

'Personal and Confidential' Mail Is Anything But

Originally Posted Tuesday, April 14, 2009

I got a letter from my health insurance company the other day.

The outside of the envelope told me that it was both "Personal and Confidential" in big and bold type.

Since this was from my health insurance company and they used very big and very bold type on the envelope to warn me that the contents were both "Personal" and "Confidential," I was immediately concerned.

Had my insurance records been broached? Was some hacker hoodlum scattering my personal health information across the Internet willy-nilly?

Or did I have some disease that I was not yet aware of, but my omnipotent insurance company had detected and was just letting me know that they considered it a pre-existing condition which they weren't going to cover. Oh, and to have a nice day.

Or was I experiencing a moment like Bruce Willis had in the movie *The Sixth Sense*, and was going to find out that I had actually died – possibly even from the disease that I didn't know I had – and my insurance company was informing me that I was no longer going to have to pay my premiums. I guess there is an upside to being dead.

So anyhow, all of those paranoid thoughts flashed through my head as I tore open the envelope and quickly scanned its contents.

"Dear Valued Member" the enclosed letter started.

My fears quickly disappeared only to be replaced by disgust. No one starts an actual "Personal" message with "Dear Valued Member."

This official looking document from my insurance company was in fact an advertisement for Zyrtec and Visine-A. The only thing "Personal" about the whole mailing was the fact they had my name and address printed on it.

And I guess I've blown the whole "Confidential" part by writing about this on my blog.

Whoops!

I'm not really sure who I'm not supposed to tell, but if they say this advertising is "Confidential" then by golly it's confidential and I won't say another word about it or at least not until I'm finished with this particular blog. Then my lips will be sealed.

I scanned through the document and noticed near the bottom in bold – but not so big – type that this junk mail – my words, not theirs – had been funded by the corporation that makes Zyrtec and Visine. No surprises there.

In the same paragraph, it enlightened me that "no patient information" had been provided to that corporation. That was a relief.

And below that paragraph – after a sentence telling me that this advertising was meant to be educational and should not be considered medical advice and after that there was another that recommended I consult a physician for any specific treatment options and then a third telling me that my insurance company and the drug company neither endorsed nor were responsible for the other's portion of this mailing – was a note informing me that if I wished to NOT receive any of these future junk-mailing – again my words, not theirs – that I could call the provided phone number.

Not only was that sentence buried deep within the fine print, the type was neither big nor bold.

I guess they were trying to keep that phone number confidential.

'Bazooka Joe' Covertly Corrupting Our Youth

Originally Posted Monday, April 19, 2010

While working on a co-worker's computer the other day, I noticed something at her desk so appalling that it could explain why the country has slowly been going to Hell-in-a-hand-basket for nearly the last 60 years.

Pinned to the corkboard by her computer were several comic strips that come with the Bazooka-brand bubblegum. I asked her about them and she said these were the funniest ones she found in her packs of gum, so she had decided to keep them.

There's nothing too unusual about that, but while waiting for her computer to restart I observed a couple of insidious facts about these seemingly harmless bubble gum comics starting with the name of the comic:

Bazooka Joe and His Gang.

Bazooka Joe comics have been around since the 1950s. While they might first appear to be harmless fun, do you have any idea the kind of message that this comic strip is giving the impressionable youth that are chewing this brand of bubble gum?

First of all, just consider the name of the main character of this comic. Bazooka.

And what is a bazooka? A great big gun, that's what. Children that chew this brand of gum and read this comic could believe that being armed with a weapon capable of disabling a tank is cool.

And since everyone knows that lessons and impressions learned at an early age tend to stick with you, when those children became teenagers they would think back to their halcyon days of chewing bubble gum and reading the Bazooka Joe comics and think to themselves, "Bazooka Joe was cool. I could use a bazooka so I can be cool too, just like Joe."

But since a bazooka is not the easiest weapon to come by, those teenagers would settle for the next best thing like AK-47s or Uzis or whatever pistol they could lay their hands on.

Which brings us to the second half of the comic strip's name:

Bazooka Joe and <u>His Gang</u>

Did you know that before the 1950s, the only gang that existed was *The Little Rascals?* I read that on the Internet, so it must be true. Just Spanky and Alfalfa and Buckwheat and the rest of the "He-Man Women Haters Club." Did they have any bazookas or AK-47s? No. Did you ever see Buckwheat try to "pop a cap" into the neighborhood "rich kid?" Of course, not.

But then along came the 1950s and Bazooka Joe and <u>His Gang</u> and practically overnight the Hells Angels and the Crips and the Bloods and dozens of other gangs were wreaking havoc in our country's largest cities.

I feel we can blame this proliferation of gun-toting gangs squarely on Bazooka-brand bubblegum and their comic Bazooka Joe.

This madness has got to stop.

It is only a matter of time before enough gum-chewing kiddies here in the Heartland grow up thinking it is OK to be in a gang. Bazooka-brand bubblegum and its "message" has to be silenced for the good of the country.

I'm not saying that we put them out of business. They just need to change the name of their comic.

For instance, how about *Basketball Joe and His Swell Bunch of Pals?* That would be acceptable. That would quit giving kids the impression that it's cool to be a gun-carrying member of a gang.

It's time to stop our country from going to Beelzebub-in-a-bubblegum-pack.

I Am No Longer A 'Blogger'

Originally Posted Friday, January 29, 2010

I am no longer a "blogger."

Now, don't get me wrong. I'm still going to write these little riffs. I'm just not going to be a "blogger." To be honest, I've never particularly liked that word.

The word "blog" has always reminded me of that one night back in the fall of 1989 when during a personal tribute to the passing of St. Louis brewery patriarch Gussie Busch, I consumed too many A-B products.

I was attempting to partake in one of every brew made by Anheuser-Busch. In case you didn't realize this, that brewery makes a <u>whole lot</u> of different products.

I blogged a couple of times that night. And the hangover the next morning was horrendous.

While I've never been a big fan of the word "blogger," I've tolerated it. After all, my big old head appears on the *Southeast Missourian* website under a category that says "Latest Blogs." By default that makes me a blogger, right?

So, a few months ago I published a blog on how to write a blog. I suppose that could be considered a wee bit narcissistic if I hadn't written it in jest. Anyhow, one of the comments I got regarding that particular blog was from a poster with the screen name of CapeCounty. The poster said:

The first thing you have to do in order to be a successful blogger is that you have to be a huge whiner, sarcastic, egomaniac, condescending, close minded bully. You really don't need to take any courses to find this out. Just read the blogs on SEMissourian. Granted this is a minority of the bloggers but they think they speak for the majority. I think they should teach or push for bloggers to state their real name and not a login name in these classes. Then we would see how opinionated they are. That would be great!

After reading the first sentence I thought, "Wow! When did I wee in his Wheaties?"

Oh sure, it was definitely possible that I had yanked the tail of a 'sacred cow' that that poster held near and dear to his heart. I can also certainly whine when I need to, and I have been known to be a wee-bit sarcastic at times, although I don't think I'm an egomaniac, condescending or close-minded. I have my opinion and you have yours and in the grand scheme of things neither really matter. Sad, but true.

But then it occurred to me upon reading the entire post, that CapeCounty was likely talking about other posters who make comments on this website behind anonymous screen names.

None of this website's <u>regular</u> bloggers are anonymous. Those are the ones whose actual mug shots and actual names run along with their writing. There are a few exceptions where the writers have used images of their subject matter rather than of themselves, but they're the minority.

However, all of the "bloggers" who post comments to stories and the named blogger's entries are essentially anonymous, writing posts using their particular screen names. I call them "posters."

Anyhow, I've read some of the poster's comments where they complement one another on a "good blog." Sometimes these comments are very well written rebuttals to something that has appeared on our website. I've even had a few comments from posters about my blogs that were actually longer than the blog I had written in the first place. Hard to believe since I can sometimes be pretty long winded.

But are they really a "blog" if you don't post your name? Should "blogger" be synonymous for a "poster?"

Personally, I don't think so. I think there is a difference between writing a blog branded with your name and your picture versus writing a post with a nom de plume.

However, I realize that I am in the minority. The term "blog" and "blogger" has become ubiquitous for ANY opinion or continuing commentary or topic discussion that appears on the Internet.

From the lady who decided to cook every recipe from Julia Child's *Mastering the Art of French Cooking* and write about it on the web to practically every celebrity documenting the minutiae of their day for excited fans to the anonymous poster on this website chastising other posters on the same website for being overly-outspoken because of their anonymity, they're all considered bloggers.

And I realize that what I think is not going to change that.

But nobody says I have to like it. As I said, I never liked the word "blog" or "blogger," but what would be a good name to call these riffs that I write?

So I thought about it.

Months went by.

No kidding. I actually wrote most of this blog in October, but was stumped for a solution to this problem.

And then the other night while attending a cycling class at Healthpoint Fitness where task-master Geoff was making us sweat our butts off, the answer came to me.

A lot of my blogs tend to take the opposite view of The Establishment. There's a lot of dumb stuff that is done in the name of "The Greater Good" and I like to point out that it is dumb and why it is dumb. Personally, I think it's fun to tweak the nose of The Man even though The Man probably doesn't find it funny.

I also have a fondness for acronyms partly because The Establishment seems to have a love of them as well. It appears to me that governments and institutions often spend more time coming up with a clever-sounding acronym rather than a truly viable solution to the problem the acronym's program is meant to be solving.

Remember T.A.R.P.? Now, that was a great solution.

So anyhow, these two facts about this "blog" and myself collided and the answer

I'd been mulling about for months came to me in a flash.

I can now say that I am no longer a blogger.

I am now Brad Insulting The Conventional Hierarchy.

Being known as a "bitcher" just seems more appropriate.

Where Does Pepperoni Come From?

Originally Posted Tuesday, April 21, 2009

I was craving a pizza the other evening.

My wife was out of town on a business trip so I was batching it. I had taken the day off from work to make some progress on renovating the last six sets of windows from my front porch and I wanted some pie, some pizza pie.

Renovating these windows has been a fairly grueling affair and I've tackled the project in spurts. Basically it has involved stripping the windows down to the bare wood, making any needed repairs then re-glazing each pair's twenty panes of glass before applying a fresh coat of primer and paint.

The eight sets of windows I've done so far look like new – there were a total of fourteen – but it's tedious work and standing on concrete for hours can make for an achy back.

So I wanted a pizza to celebrate my progress.

I considered ordering one, but since we were out of orange juice I figured I would just dash over to the local grocery store and kill two birds with one stone. The OJ was a quick buy, but the pizza took a little longer to choose.

Did I want the California Pizza Kitchen BBQ Chicken pizza which is pretty good, but definitely not as tasty as eating it in one of their actual restaurants or did I want one of those thick crust pizzas that take nearly a half-hour to bake or did I want a nice, quick-to-cook Tony's pizza that I often consumed when I was still a bachelor?

Tony's won out of sentimental reasons and I took a pepperoni pie home with me for a quick bake and a quicker devouring.

While the oven was heating up, I noticed on the front of the box that my pizza was topped with "Pepperoni Made With Pork, Chicken and Beef."

While I have eaten pepperoni pizza for years, I've never considered where the meat came from. I certainly never thought it came from a pig, a chicken and a cow. Reading that on the box reminded me of that odd Thanksgiving entrée, the turducken, which is a duck stuffed inside a chicken that is then stuffed inside a turkey.

Could the pepperoni on my pizza be the result of a cowpigen – a chicken stuffed inside a pig which is then stuffed inside a cow? And how long would it take to cook something that huge? Days, I imagine.

But then reality sunk in. I realized that this innocuous sounding marketing spin was a veiled way of saying that all of the marginal parts of slaughtered cows, pigs and chickens were shipped to a sausage maker who ground them all up and made pepperoni for the pie I was getting ready to nosh on.

Yum.

In junior high I read the book *The Jungle* by Upton Sinclair. It documented the deplorable conditions in the Chicago meatpacking industry around 1905. After reading the vivid and often disgusting descriptions in that book, I briefly became a vegetarian. Of course after a week of Pop Tarts and salad, I pushed the book's descriptions from the forefront of my mind and found a hamburger to devour.

Now that I'm older, details like those penned by Upton Sinclair and the thought of the possible existence of a cowpigen still stifle my appetite, just not for a week.

More like the 11 to 13 minutes it takes to actually bake the pizza.

Don't Like A Definition? Try a Different Dictionary.

Originally Posted Friday, April 24, 2009

When writing one of my blogs, I often use online dictionaries and thesauruses to verify the meaning of a word or find a synonym.

I could get my butt out of my easy chair and go all the way to my second floor office where we keep our dictionary and thesaurus, but that is way too much work. Going online is a lot easier.

I was writing a blog not long ago, where I used the word "memories." I wanted a synonym for the word, but didn't know one off the top of my head. I was experiencing what neuro-scientists call a "brain-fart."

So I looked up the word "memories" and discovered that the online dictionary I use has a fairly grim definition of what I've always considered a fairly innocuous word.

Memories is a "reminder of death" is how it defined the word.

Some of the synonyms listed included "death's-head," "reminder of human failure," "reminder of mortality," and "skull."

I didn't know "memories," was such a depressing word.

The definition given online was so depressing that I forced myself out of my chair and up to our second-floor office to double-check it against my ever-so-trusty 1971 edition of *The American Heritage Dictionary of the English Language.*

The book's definitions were much more pleasant.

None of the 10 definitions it listed were anywhere close to being as apocalyptic as the online dictionary.

For instance, one of the definitions in the book was:

"An act or instance of remembrance; a recollection: 'He fell into pleasant memories of his childhood.'"

That was much better.

The synonyms listed in my 1971 dictionary were also nowhere near as grim as the ones I found online.

They included "memory," "remembrance," "recollection," "reminiscence," and "retrospect." There wasn't any mention of "death's-heads" or "human failure."

Just reading the definition and synonyms from my *American Heritage Dictionary* immediately conjured up memories of stomping through freshly-raked piles of leaves as a rambunctious 4-year-old and playing T-ball on hot summer days and as a teenager floating down the Mississippi with my friend Jim on our home-built raft, trying to make it to Cairo where we could catch a steamship up the Ohio River and into the free states. Yes, those were the days.

You know, that's the funny thing about memories. Sometimes things you read or that you watch on TV morph into a memory that you would swear is true, that you had those experiences. It's actually just your mind playing tricks on you. It happens to me sometimes.

For instance, I re-read that last paragraph, and realized that I never, ever played T-ball growing up.

Not once.

Getting Rid of Grandpa Franklin

Originally Posted Monday, March 29, 2010

We had a rough weekend.

The family decided that it was finally time to get rid of Grandpa Franklin.

We all know we should respect our elders, but there comes a time and place where – from an unemotional business standpoint – the return on investment just isn't there.

Grandpa Franklin has had his day in the sun, looming large over all the kids through out the years, but now at 83 he's really showing his age.

First of all, he's a little shaky. We think he might have Parkinson's disease. Or it could be his hip. He's complained about it for years. He wants the family to help him pay for a new one. Have you any idea how expensive one of those titanium joints cost?

Heck, it would practically bankrupt the family to pay for all the care needed to make Grandpa Franklin stable again. But a lot of the grownups are scared silly he might just collapse at anytime and crush one or two of the grandkids with him. We feel we can't take that chance.

And let's be honest, even if we replace his hip what do we have then? Same old Grandpa who's a little more stable who will probably pass on in a couple of years. It almost doesn't seem worth it.

And then there is the whole incontinence problem. Why else would he keep that box of Depends on his dresser? Yes, the family knows that Grandpa Franklin leaking is not fatal and it can be controlled. Obviously, he's doing his best with Depends, but still it's kind of embarrassing to all the grandkids.

Who wants to be known as the kid with a leaky Grandpa?

And this might sound a bit selfish, but let's just say what needs to be said:

Grandpa Franklin is just no longer cool.

The grandkids want a grandpa who knows about things like the Internet and IPods and Lady Gaga. They don't care about rotary phones and how it was like living through the Great Depression and the Cold War.

Other kids have cooler, younger Grandpas. There's Grandpa Clippard and Grandpa Schrader. They're all younger and hip. Even Grandpa Jefferson and Grandpa Blanchard, who might not be quite as cool as the others at least don't have to run around in Depends.

And remember Grandpa Schultz? Now there's a piece of work. Everyone pretty much wrote him off for dead because the "experts" said it was so and everyone believed them. But I saw him just the other day on Pacific and he was looking sharp. Even had a lady on each arm. I hope I'm that spry when I'm 95.

So as far as Grandpa Franklin is concerned, the family has decided to use the old tried and true raccoon-relocation-routine and haul him over to the first busy truck stop we can find in Southern Illinois. We will leave him without his wallet at a booth sipping coffee and rambling on to himself like he tends to do while we slip off back to Cape.

We're confident that within a few hours some nice Illinois state trooper will be called in and when Grandpa starts babbling on about how "in his day, kids walked miles up hill both ways barefoot in snow to see him" that he'll be gently led off to a nicer place that can deal with his shakiness and his incontinence.

And then the family can get a cooler Grandpa Franklin who knows about things like the Internet and Ipods.

Perhaps, our new Grandpa Franklin might even be able to explain to me what's so darn cool about Lady Gaga.

Soda Additives Anonymous

Originally Posted Tuesday, April 27, 2010

"I'd like to welcome Brad to this meeting. This is his first visit to Soda Additives Anonymous."

A dozen voices chorused the sentiment.

"Brad would you like to share some things about yourself with the group?"

"Uh, yes. I've been something of a soda addict for years. I first got hooked when 7-11 introduced the Big Gulp in 1980. But at first it was just soda, just lots and lots of soda. Diet Pepsi mostly. I was fine with that for years.

"But one time I was going through the drive-through at the Keg Shoppe on Independence and they had a sign in the window saying I could add vanilla to my soda for just 15 cents more. So I thought I'd try it. And I found I liked it. I really, really liked it.

"Soon I was visiting them every other day getting a soda and squirt of that delicious extract. But then one squirt wasn't enough, so I'd start buying two squirts.

"Then the Keg Shoppe closed, and I didn't know where to turn to. Barnes and Noble carried some vanilla syrup and I bought a bottle, but it just wasn't the same. Then I found out that Kidd's on Kingshighway had vanilla syrup and I started going through their drive-thru.

"I thought I had my addiction under control. I was happy to go to Kidd's just a couple times a week for a fix. But then one day I was getting gas at the Rhodes on William, and noticed back at their soda fountains that they had vanilla and cherry extracts... on tap. I could put in as much as I wanted into my soda for no extra charge.

"So I made a Coke-Zero and put in a couple squirts of vanilla. It was soooo good. I went back the next day for another... and then, the day after that. I had to have my daily fix. Sometime I even stopped by a couple times a day. I couldn't control myself.

"At first I was OK with just a couple squirts. But then it started losing its edge. I started putting in more squirts. Two squirts became three. Three became a four. Soon I was paying neighborhood kids to distract the clerks at Rhodes so I could 'beer bong' some of that delicious syrup right from the tap.

"I need help.

"My name is Brad and I'm a soda additives addict."

It's Tough To Legislate Ugly

Posted Monday, July 20, 2009

It occurred to me the other day, how tough it is to legislate ugly.

Now for the sake of this essay, when I refer to ugly, I'm not talking about people. One person's hottie is another person's nottie. For instance, I think Paris Hilton is one of the skankiest women alive today, and I wouldn't cross the street to meet her. But some guys think she is to die for.

No, for this discussion, I'm using the term to pertain specifically to property. And ugly properties are tough to legislate.

How many times have you driven by a house painted with atrocious colors and said to yourself, "There ought to be a law against something like that?" I'm sure I've done it dozens of times. Eye-sores are apparent to everyone except the people who are the eye-sorees. In the case of a godawful paint job, maybe the owners are color blind. Or perhaps they got some paint on sale.

There used to be a house in Hatyi on the main drag that was painted a very royal purple. It actually may still be there, but I haven't been that way in several years. To me, it was a Very Ugly House. But I bet that the owners of that property both loved that color and loved coming home every night to that glorious, bright purple.

However, passer-bys like me would just cringe and think about legislating ugly, which as I said is pretty darn tough.

And the reason it's tough is because it's a freedom of expression issue and the last time I checked that was protected by the U.S. Constitution.

While a purple house might be an eyesore to 99.99% of the population, the only offense it suffers from is bad taste. But unless you live in a modern subdivision with covenants, conditions and restrictions (CC&Rs) typically nothing can be done.

CC&Rs are the bylaws that homeowners of given subdivisions must abide by and those rules can dictate everything you can do with your property up to and including good taste in the form of specific paint colors which you may or may not use to paint the exterior of your house.

I've never lived in a subdivision with CC&Rs. I've read about them. It sounds a little communistic, if you ask me, but I'd probably do the same thing if I had the opportunity to create my own subdivision from scratch. Communism isn't so bad if you're the one in charge.

First of all, my subdivision would have to have a catchy name that stood out. I've noticed that local subdivisions often include some kind of a tree in their name. Cedar and Oak are popular, but frankly I think they're a little over-used. It also helps to have a verb in the name.

I like Thundering Thorny Locust Estates.

Hah! You probably thought I would call it something like Bradivision or Bradfield or Bradland Hills. Well, I'm not that egotistical. I would just use my name for a street or two, such as Brad Boulevard, Brad Avenue, Brad Drive, Brad Promenade, Brad Thoroughfare, Bradway and the Hollerbach Turnpike.

While you think I might be a little ridiculous with this naming convention, I'm only exaggerating a smidge. Some friends of mine live in "Castle Pines," a west St. Louis county subdivision where every street has the word "Castle" in the name.

I'm pretty sure their subdivision also have CC&Rs.

The last time I visited them, there wasn't a purple house anywhere in sight.

Dear Doofus Who Rented "The DaVinci Code" Before Me

I would like to know what the heck you did with this DVD besides watching it.

Even though I cleaned the disk with a soft cloth – this is something I do every time I watch a DVD since I've come to learn that unless it is brand-new and fresh out of the cellophane, there will be blemishes of some kind – this video paused every 10 seconds.

It skipped chapters. It pixelized on screen. It stuttered. It made me wistful for VHS tapes.

I attempted to watch the movie for 15 minutes thinking that the problem might just be with the first couple chapters, but finally gave up in utter disgust.

Let me take this opportunity to explain the steps in renting and using a DVD because you apparently do not grasp them.

First, you rent the DVD and take it home.

At home – right before you're getting ready to watch it – you press the little black knob in the center of the DVD case which helps release the disk locking mechanism.

Next, you gently – repeat after me, *gently* – pop it out of its case using your fingers. If you feel you have to use a spork or some other handy eating instrument to assist, you're doing it wrong.

After you have removed the DVD from its case, handle it using your fingertips and the edges of the disk and carefully place it into your DVD player. If you are like me, just prior to this step, you may clean the DVD with a soft cloth.

Do not use steel wool and Spic-n-Span as you apparently decided was a good choice with this particular video.

Also, you may not be aware that the case which a DVD comes in, is its little house, and it is something of a homebody. If the DVD is not in your DVD player, then it should be kept in its little house. It likes it there.

It should NOT be used as a Frisbee or a coaster for your Milwaukee's Best beer or a handy place to set that wayward nacho or a makeshift toothpick or back-scratcher or an impromptu play toy for either your child or your pet.

And you should not take the DVD out of its case – remember, it is a homebody – and leave it out loose on your coffee table days before you are planning on watching it.

And while this letter is meant to make you aware of proper DVD etiquette, you may also want to reflect on your diet while you are at it.

Based on the quality of the fingerprints you left on the DVD, you should seriously consider reducing your intake of fatty foods. Your pores appear to be oozing oil. If you keep stuffing gobs of greasy-goodness down your pie-hole, then I imagine you won't be around very long to enjoy renting other DVDs in the future including

Angels & Demons, the upcoming prequel to *The DaVinci Code*.

KFC 'Honey' Is Not What It Seems

Originally Posted Wednesday, May 12, 2010

The other evening it was my night to cook so I got dinner from KFC along with some packets of "honey" to top off my biscuits.

When I arrived home I noticed that what I thought was honey was actually something that KFC calls "honey sauce." This struck me as odd. Isn't honey already a sauce, courtesy of Mother Nature? I glanced at the ingredients.

Mother Nature's sole ingredient in honey is, well, honey. But that's not the case with "honey sauce" from KFC.

Honey was actually the 4th ingredient, right behind "sugar" and "corn syrup." The main ingredient was "high fructose corn syrup" or HFCS. Kind of made me think that KFC should have named this "High Fructose Corn Syrup Sauce." I guess Honey Sauce sounds better.

While TV surfing a few months ago, I came upon a program that discussed all the uses of HFCS. The ingredient is used everywhere, from soda to bread to salad dressings to even the can of Campbell's Light Chicken with Wild Rice Soup that is in our pantry.

There are two primary reasons why High Fructose Corn Syrup is used in so many products. It's a preservative that extends the shelf life of processed foods and it is cheaper than sugar.

Considering it is a preservative and the quantities that most American's – myself included – consume products containing HFCS, it does make one wonder what it will do to our bodies once we have passed on.

Will archaeologists a thousand years from now exhume our remains and remark about how well preserved they are? Will they debate whether the reason is due to 21st century embalming techniques or from a diet high in HFCS?

I guess only time will tell. You can mull that one over the next time you're enjoying some ice-cold beer sauce.

TPing In The Good Ol' Days

Originally Posted Friday, May 21, 2010

Recently while going to work, I passed by a house that had been tee-peed. You don't see that too often any more. Guess it requires hard work and the members of this younger generation just aren't up for the exercise or have the work ethic.

Ahhhh, yes, that reminds me of the good ol' days...

Tell us more, Grandpa!

Yes, I remember when growing up that houses covered with toilet paper were a regular sight in the mornings. Perhaps, it was because toilet paper was cheap back then. Only a nickel a roll – even for the "good stuff"– and anybody could buy it.

Teenagers would walk into the local five-and-dime with a couple bucks and come out with a case of Northern. If the cashier even looked a bit quizzical, most kids would just flash them a pained grimace and whisper "Bad Mexican" and that was a good enough explanation.

But then somebody must have complained to the right person and one thing led to another and suddenly what once was a nickel a roll shot up 10-fold! The "good stuff" was even more!

TPing was no longer the inexpensive entertainment for the younger generation it had once been. While homeowners everywhere rejoiced that they would no longer have to figure out how to pluck a piece of quilted Charmin from a limb 20 feet off the ground, a part of American traditions fell by the wayside, apparently destroyed by its own success and basic economics.

But it's nice to see that some youngsters haven't completely forgotten about the old rites. Perhaps, their parents or grandparents told them stories of how they could hurl a roll of Cottonelle over a house when they were younger.

Or maybe the kids were playing Wii TP and decided to try their luck with the real thing.

Or possibly, whomever tee-peed this particular house, saw a package of toilet paper and said to his or her self, "I think I'm going to go decorate the outside of so-and-so's house with these rolls of tissue paper" thinking it was a completely original idea.

I don't know what the inspiration was, but it made me wax sentimental.

And be thankful it wasn't my house that got tee-peed.

A Surplus Of Left-Handed Work Gloves

Originally Posted Friday, May 28, 2010

I have an over-abundance of left-handed work gloves.

I noticed this recently while preparing to weed some flowerbeds. I grabbed what I thought was a set of gloves out of my garage, but quickly discovered that they were both lefties.

This is not an un-common occurrence for me. Since I am right-handed, holes always first appear on my right gloves. I tend to use them until the holes become too big, then I pitch the right glove leaving a left-handed glove in very good shape to sit on a shelf in my garage. I've collected a small pile of these solitary gloves.

In a pinch, I've been known to use a left-handed glove on my right hand. It's not very comfortable and I don't like to do it for long, but it's better than no glove at all if – for instance – you need to remove poison ivy from a flowerbed.

While the rule of "leaves of 3, let it be" may be accurate if you're hiking in the woods, when the poisonous plant shows up in my yard, I come out with guns-a-blazing, or more appropriately gloves-a-pulling.

I tend to buy gloves that I have found work well for the chosen task. Some types of gloves I just don't like. For instance, I really don't care for common brown jersey gloves. When I've used them, they leave my fingers covered in a blackish cotton fuzz. They also offer practically no protection against splinters. Besides that, they wear out fast.

I like to buy gloves that will last a while. I'm partial to leather that is not so stiff you can't move your fingers, but not so soft you could blow your nose in them. And obviously the amount of time a pair of gloves will last greatly depends on what I will be doing with them. If the gloves are for gripping the lawnmower or weeding flowerbeds, I feel they ought to last from spring to fall.

However, if I'm laying pavers or digging postholes by hand I realize that no matter how expensive the gloves are, their life expectancy will be significantly shorter.

Or at least my right glove will be. It never fails.

The Never-Ending War

Originally Posted Friday, July 09, 2010

The war is back on.

I've been waging it for 16 years and there is no end in sight. This war is my Iraq, my Afghanistan. I have no exit strategy. There is just an enemy that can't seem to be killed. All I can do is keep it at bay.

During the winter the enemy is usually quiet. But when the spring rains trickle off leaving behind the humidity and heat that is Southeast Missouri in the summer, the enemy attacks, and attacks hard.

The enemy is a vine.

But it is not just any old vine. It is The Vine and I am convinced that it can't be killed.

The Vine typically appears in May, popping up in the various flowerbeds around my house. Sometimes it will even show up in the middle of my zoysia turf. Trying to dig it up is pointless. The Vine tends to snap off just inches below the surface and like a dandelion, it re-appears a week later in the same place.

Chemicals don't seem to faze The Vine. Round-Up will kill everything around The Vine, but The Vine itself doesn't even wilt. Even Triox – the weed killer for those wishing to pursue a "scorched-earth" policy of weed management – doesn't affect it.

I'm not sure where The Vine came from. I think it is some kind of mutant hybrid that probably originated at the house next to ours. Mrs. Brentlinger lived there for almost 70 years and had an affinity for aggressive and invasive plants. English ivy. Mint. Honeysuckle. Yucca. Wisteria. Somehow they all coexisted in her yard, each with their own little fiefdom.

My wife and I bought her house about 10 years ago and we've gradually tamed and contained her landscaping.

The mint got dug up. I corralled the English ivy with a stair-stepping wooden wall that follows the slope of the yard. The honeysuckle eventually succumbed to repeated hacking. We've learned that the wisteria needs a vicious haircut at least twice a year. But apparently the yucca plants can't be killed. I have tried, but a heavy dose of Triox only seemed to make them come back bigger.

I'm convinced that somehow the yucca and the English ivy crossbred at some point in time resulting in The Vine. It is the only reasonable explanation that could explain this weed's sheer tenacity.

It just can't be killed. It is The Terminator. If it could climb inside a Mac truck and use a stick-shift, I'm sure it would try to run me down. It knows I'm a threat and even though I have not been successful at killing it. I think I may be the only thing that stands between The Vine and Armageddon.

The war is back on, and I pray for winter to return soon.

The Canadians Are Coming! The Canadians Are Coming!

Originally Posted Friday, July 17, 2009

Back in January, I recounted in this blog that Russian Professor Igor Panarin was predicting that the U.S would go through a civil war this fall and split up into 6 different republics by the summer of 2010.

The professor believed that Missouri – along with Illinois and Kansas and all the states directly north of us, would become part of the Central Northern American Republic and likely be part of Canada.

I've been watching the news and preparing for this potential event ever since I wrote about it since there is a lot to do before a civil war.

There are snacks to buy. You need plenty of beer. A must-have is a 100-inch TV so you can watch all the action as it unfolds live on the cable news networks. Oh, and you have to have guns and lots and lots of ammo, just in case you need to protect that 100-inch TV from looters.

I'm mostly prepared. I still need to get the guns and ammo. Currently, the only gun I have is a Super Soaker from Hasbro. While it may not be lethal, I can assure you that it will not only get you pretty darn wet, that under very specific conditions it could even shoot somebody's eye out.

So anyhow, I've been scanning the headlines since January and I think I now have empirical evidence of the impending war. I don't want to get you all panicky, but I think everyone should know this fact:

THE CANADIANS ARE COMING! THE CANADIANS ARE COMING!

I think Professor Panarin got part of his prediction wrong. Oh sure, we're going to become part of Canada all right, but it's not going to be from our own choice. They're invading and they're invading NOW!

Those wily Canadians have had their eyes on Missouri and our little corner of the Heartland for quite sometime. As evidence, I give you the airport. Actually the city might just give you the airport if you asked nicely and agreed to take over the various debt payments associated with that property, but that is another story.

Anyhow, you have to look no further than the airport to figure out that those Canadians have been coveting our corner of the Heartland for quite sometime. Just look at the recent sale of the Commander Premier outfit. Who bought it? Canadians, that's who.

According to my friend Paranoid Pete, Canada initially planned to invade our country back in 1999. Pete heard about it from a guy who heard it from another guy who overheard a couple of other guys talking about it while visiting the restroom at Buffalo Wild Wings in the Town Plaza. With a pedigree like that, this story must be true.

"So back in 1999 a company called Zenair chose Cape Girardeau to reputedly make a plane," Pete told me. "This was all just a cover story. In fact, Cape was going to be Canada's southern-most beachhead – or perhaps considering our geography, bootheelhead – for their conquest of middle America. But then the Canadians found out that George W. Bush was going to be elected in 2000 over Al Gore and they postponed the invasion."

"Wait a second, Pete. I read about Zenair. They pulled out of coming to Cape in May 1999. That's like 18 months BEFORE Bush was elected to office."

"Yeah, so what? The Canadians have great intel. Everybody knows that. They just want you to think they're all milquetoast."

"OK. So let's say Canada was going to invade the United States in 1999 and let's say they actually knew the outcome of our 2000 presidential election 18 months before it was actually held, then why did they cancel their plan just because of George W?"

"It's really simple. George W scared the bejesus out of Canada. They knew he was a cowboy and they knew if they'd already invaded the US that as president he would have come after them loaded for bear. Basically, they were terrified that he might nuke them in retaliation, so they backed off and decided to wait until someone not so ballsy was in office."

"Like Obama?"

"Exactly."

Sometime my friend Paranoid Pete does not sound so paranoid and actually makes sense in a distorted world-view kind of way. This was one of those times.

In fact, after giving Pete's story some serious consideration, I think it may be likely that the Mayor of Cape is even in on the invasion.

Shocking, I know, but Knutson is from Minnesota, which everyone knows is practically South Canada. I believe he's a mole sent here years ago to infiltrate the upper-echelon of Southeast Missouri high society.

Don't think that idea is so far-fetched. Hitler reputedly did stuff like that leading up to the outbreak of World War Two. And that's not the only similarity.

Germany had Blitzkrieg where legions of tanks and infantry swept into neighboring countries. Canada will have Canuckkrieg and use heavily armored snowmobiles to sweep down into Middle America. Or at least that's what Paranoid Pete told me.

Of course the question on everyone's mind is why. Why would Canada want to invade the Heartland of the United States?

It's supply and demand, my friends. They need resources that we have and it's not oil. Unlike ourselves who consume about 25% of the world's petroleum production, Canada has plenty of that.

But we have pigs and the Canadians want them. No kidding. I read it in the *Wall Street Journal*.

Global warming has resulted in skinnier Canadian pigs. Skinnier pigs means that they are producing both less and less tasty back-bacon.

And everyone who has ever watched the documentary *Strange Brew* knows, Canadians love their back-bacon. With their supply of back-bacon in danger of drying up they set their sights on the figurative Saudi Arabia of Pork – Iowa – and all of the other pork producing states around it. That includes Missouri.

In fact 6 of the top 7 pork-producing states are in the Canadian invasion plan. If it succeeds, they will have at least hundred year supply of back-bacon.

So watch out if an Artic Clipper buries the Midwest this coming winter with snow down to the Arkansas line because the only sure thing that will stop an endless wave of back-bacon starved, heavily-armed, snow-mobile riding Canadians is no snow.

And maybe my trusty Super Soaker.

Did I mention it can shoot an eye out?

The Forecast Calls For.... A Tsunami????

Originally Posted Wednesday, August 12, 2009

When storms blew through the area last Tuesday, I got five or six text messages on my phone from the *Southeast Missourian* website alerting me of various weather warnings throughout the evening.

With the exception of one flash-flood warning, I essentially got all of the alerts <u>after</u> they had already expired. One was *almost two hours* after the fact.

Damn, that lousy, stinkin', good-for-nothin' newspaper website!

Oh, wait! I work at that lousy, stinkin', good-for-nothin' newspaper and I'm neck-deep in the technology side, so I guess there must have been a good reason for the delay. But as a consumer and a customer myself of the newspaper website, I certainly didn't like it. I want my weather information in a timely manner, that's why I signed up for weather alerts at SEMissourian.com.

So, I started investigating the situation and it appears to have been caused by some kind of a bottleneck on the AT&T wireless network. Other employees at the paper who also use AT&T noticed the same untimely nature of our weather alerts.

However, our token Verizon user – online editor Matt Sanders – got the same weather information in a timely manner.

This appears to be a pretty easy fix. Everyone who currently uses AT&T for wireless, cancel your contract and switch to Verizon.

Problem solved.

While I was looking into this issue, I decided to check the weather alert options of some of the other area media.

I first signed up for the local CBS affiliate's weather alerts. However, they don't offer text-messaging, just email. That's fine if you have a smart-phone with email access.

I do, but I don't want it to squawk at me every time a piece of email shows up. If I did that, it would be yelping all the time, so that function of my phone stays in silent mode. But I do have incoming text messages sound an alarm. I don't get many of them and the ones that I do receive are either weather-related or letting me know what restaurant my wife and I should meet our friends Mark and Claire at for happy hour. In other words, critical stuff.

I next visited the local NBC affiliate's website. Reputedly, they have text messaging weather alerts, but their system kept giving me an error whenever I tried to sign up that service.

However, I was able to sign up for their email weather alerts where I encountered something... unusual.

The NBC affiliate has a more customizable weather alert system than either the *Southeast Missourian* or the local CBS station. They allow users to pick which specific weather events they want to be emailed about.

Some of these are rather typical for our area. "Severe Thunderstorm," "Winter Storm," "Tornado" and "Flooding", I would expect. However, "Hurricane" I really don't think is a necessary option for anyone living in the Heartland. Any hurricane that wanders this far north has usually decayed into a thunderstorm or two by the time it gets here.

But the one that I really couldn't understand was "tsunami." I'm not joking.

Are tsunamis really a threat to *anyone* living in the Midwest? And if they are, and a wall of water 50-feet-high was headed our way, I think it's safe to say that basically we are all screwed and none of us will be worrying about the timeliness of our weather-alerts going forward.

I do rather like how NBC affiliate handles its Weather Alerts. Maybe by offering a "tsunami" alert they are zeroing in on an underserved part of the weather monitoring market that the *Southeast Missourian* website has been ignoring.

That's why, I'm going to recommend to our webmaster that we also offer our users customizable weather alerts including tsunamis. Just because I'm a doubting Thomas doesn't mean they can't happen here.

For that matter, we will also include typhoons, earthquakes, volcanic eruptions, gamma ray bursts, asteroid-collisions, locust plagues and nuclear war. Oh sure, I know some of those are a little hard to predict, but that's no reason why we can't cater to the end-of-the-world-is-near market.

I've even lined up an advertiser in case one of these apocalyptic disasters does happen to occur.

For instance, if NASA spots an asteroid heading on a collision course for the Gulf of Mexico, ChapStick will sponsor our text message alert. That's smart marketing.

We all will need a tube, so we can kiss our butt good-bye.

Whatever Happened To Quality?

Posted Monday, February 15, 2010, at 12:00 AM

I'm ticked off about my jeans.

I know there are much grander things to be ticked off about like the fact our Federal Government keeps digging this country a deficit hole which is currently two-thirds of the way through the planet and headed directly to Beijing.

It's looking grim and just to hedge my bets I've been boning up on useful Chinese phrases such as:

多少木材将一盘，如果土拨鼠土拨鼠可以夹头木材？

How much wood would a woodchuck chuck if a woodchuck could chuck wood?

While the runaway federal deficit is a worthy thing to be ticked off about, today I'm focusing my scorn on my pants.

Pants do not normally irritate me.

Usually, my pants do a bang-up job of keeping my legs warm and my paleness out-of-sight. My pants protect me from wayward rocks stirred up by my weedwacker in the summer time and when I'm crawling around refinishing a hardwood floor as I did this past fall.

Of course, I usually reserve old pants for that kind of work. Those are the pants that I've worn enough times that the cuffs are getting frayed and the openings to the pockets are showing wear.

For me old pants do not die, they just become attire to do chores around the house. Even after the pants are too tattered to be used for home maintenance work – this usually involves a Catastrophic Crotch Blow Out that sometimes happens to me when I don't use a belt and am doing a lot of bending and stretching – I use them for rags.

But I like a little time to go by between when I originally buy my pants and when I'm cutting them up into rags, preferably a couple years.

The pants I was ticked off about were showing premature wear in the calf region. They're only about 4-months-old and at this rate they're not going to last a year. The denim is looking like I've been clumsily climbing barbed wire fences. I know that some people like their pants to have that distressed, fresh-from-breaking-out-of-prison look, but that wasn't what I bought. I bought new pants that I expected to basically look new for at least a year.

Of course, I believe that our civilization reached the height of pants technology with the Toughskins jeans that Sears sold when I was a kid. Toughskins was an appropriate name. While they were made out of denim, they wore like leather.

They were also the bluest pants you've ever seen. Boys who wore them looked half-child and half-Smurf. And they never, ever faded. Not sure what kind of dye they used in those jeans – lead-based probably – but you would out-grow them before they showed any sign of wear or fading.

But today's jeans just don't compare. I realize that's business. If a company can shave a few pennies off of every unit of a given product they make by using less raw materials, the overall saving can be tremendous.

And in this case, how many customers are really going to notice that the denim used to make their jeans wasn't quite as good as it used to be?

质量低劣的痛苦仍然不久，低廉的价格甜度是遗忘。 -莱昂米考蒂洛

The bitterness of poor quality remains
long after the sweetness of cheap price is forgotten.
-- Leon M. Cautillo

Shouldn't Baristas Be Really, Really, <u>Really</u> Fast?

Originally Posted Friday, August 13, 2010

My wife had business in Denver last week, and since she was going to be returning to St. Louis late Saturday evening, I decided that I would pick her up when she arrived at the airport.

However, late evening turned into even later when she texted me that her flight was going to be delayed because of lightning around the Colorado airport.

Considering that I was already running short on sleep and was facing a 2-hour drive home after she arrived, I felt that a caffeinated coffee beverage was in order. Since I was already browsing the books at a Borders in Brentwood, I thought I would sample something from their attached café.

I ordered a *"Hand-Shaken ColdBrewed Caramel White Latte."*

As I waited and watched the fellow behind the counter make my drink, a couple of questions came to mind:

If a drink description says it is "hand-shaken" shouldn't there be some kind of up and down movement of the arms and shoulders of the person making the drink?

And how come most baristas are so slow?

By definition, baristas make coffee drinks. That is their job. And because that is their job, they are in close contact with coffee and coffee beans and brewing coffee and coffee grounds and... oh heck, I could go on like Bubba telling Forrest about shrimp, but you get the point.

Baristas practically wallow in all things coffee.

And yet, even with all that exposure to highly caffeinated bean-based beverages, I've observed over the years that many of them appear to be fairly slow when it comes to assembling whatever concoction a customer has ordered. It's like they've never done it before and are making the recipe for the first time.

Shouldn't a barista who has been a barista for more than a month be practically super-human fast?

Or have they become de-sensitized to the rejuvenating properties of coffee-based beverages from sheer over-exposure? Or were they practically flat-lining before they came to work and what I consider slow is in fact a certifiable miracle from them main-lining a soy-latte frappe with a triple shot of expresso at the beginning of their shift?

Perhaps, I am being harsh on this profession.

Maybe they're just being methodical. Methodical is not bad. Methodical means you're getting the job done right, the first time and every time. That is especially important when you are making something as complex as an *"Almost Hand-Shaken ColdBrewed Caramel White Latte."*

'Crop Circle' Proof Of Alien Invasion

Originally Posted Monday, August 24, 2009

I think aliens have invaded my neighborhood.

And I'm not talking about the good kind of aliens who can whip together a tasty shrimp quesadilla in a matter of minutes or always seem to be working in the background on a lot of those landscaping programs they show on HGTV. Those kinds of aliens have been in our town for quite a while.

No, I'm talking about the type of aliens that the U.S. Government snatched up in Roswell, New Mexico after a UFO crashed there in 1947. You know, little green men.

Or at least I presume, they are little green men. I definitely know the ones that landed in my neighborhood are little because I found the markings from one of their landing craft in my yard while talking to a roofing contractor the other day.

I looked down and there it was, a perfectly round circle of green grass, distinctly darker than the other grass around it.

Since I do 100% of the lawn maintenance for the Hollerbach household, I knew something was not right. I applied fertilizer in April and I know I didn't do any donuts with my drop-spreader back then. If I had, that might have caused the miniature crop circle I now have in my lawn although I doubt I could have made it exactly 7 feet in diameter.

That's how I know the little green men have to be pretty little. Seven feet is a pretty small footprint for any kind of UFO. You're not going to find Sigourney Weaver's nemesis from the movie *Alien* traveling in a spaceship that small.

Well, unless of course, that those aliens have the extraterrestrial version of the Yugo. Remember the Yugo? It was kind of like a Mini Cooper, but less spacious. Actually, a Yugo-sized spacecraft could explain why the alien in *Alien* was so damn mean. If I had to travel umpteen million light-years squeezed into a spaceship the size of a refrigerator, I'd be in a pretty foul mood whenever I reached my destination.

Ok, just so I can sleep at night and my wife won't wonder why I'm now insisting on going to bed with a Louisville Slugger tucked under my pillow, I'm going to assume that my first assumption is correct and that the crop circle in my lawn was made by little green men aliens and not by the toothy horror from *Alien* aliens.

I think I can handle little aliens. Based on the size of their spaceship's footprint, I imagine they're about 12 inches tall. As long as they don't propagate like the Tribbles from the classic episode of the original *Star Trek* series, I'll be in good shape.

In an effort to catch the little green men who apparently landed on my property, I have strategically placed a couple of traps that I've had for a few years. I originally bought them to catch some baby raccoons that took up residence under my porch and they've been stashed in my garage ever since. I have them baited with cans of beer. The alien in *E.T.* seemed to like a cold brewski so I figured that was a good use for the last of the Pomegranate Mich Ultra that was lingering in the back of my fridge. I hope aliens like flavored light beer.

Unfortunately, I've not yet caught anything. To improve my odds, I've been watching the *Outdoor Channel* to see if it might air a program with tips on hunting aliens. For example, what kind of crops to plant on your property that might attract aliens who enjoy making crop circles? So far that's been a bust, not one program on how to bag an alien. However, I now know everything there is to know about the best methods of attracting a big buck to my back yard so I'll be in great shape this coming deer season.

Besides the traps, I've been literally beating the bushes hoping to scare at least one of little green men out. So far that hasn't worked either. I'm also staying clear of the crop circle. Who knows what kind of alien voodoo caused that grass to be greener. It could be radioactive, but since I don't have a Gieger counter I really can't say.

I just hope that those lead underpants I ordered off the internet arrive before the next time I need to mow.

The Second Annual Christmas Running of the Cats

Originally Posted Monday, December 29, 2008

If it is not raining or snowing, we let our cat Patches out into our fenced-in backyard two or three times a day for 10 to 20 minutes of exercise.

We always watch her when she goes outside since Patch is fully de-clawed and can't protect herself. Or at least that's what we think.

No one has ever bothered to tell the cat that.

Patches' usual outside routine is to wander around the yard, inspecting the areas she usually inspects – the front fence row, behind the garage, the nooks behind the clumps of pampas grass – occasionally stalking a bird or a squirrel and generally being on the lookout for her Arch-Enemy Smokey.

Smokey is a short-haired, gray female cat which belongs to our tenants next door. Smokey is part-indoor, but mostly outdoor cat who our cat simply HATES. Whenever the two happen to meet in our yard, we always try to sweep up Patches as fast as possible because she is always the aggressor, claws or not.

I guess in the cat world, weapons like claws and teeth are important, but attitude trumps them both.

Patches has plenty of 'tude.

Last Christmas, Patches spied Smokey in our backyard and promptly chased her out an open gate and down to the street. That almost gave both my wife and I cardiac episodes.

We did not want to duplicate that incident for Christmas this year.

But as I was getting ready to let Patches out in her backyard on Christmas morning this year, I spied Smokey stranded on the neighbor's garage roof. I'm not sure how she got up there, but apparently she could not figure out how to get down.

Using a long board I got her to walk over to our fence. She quickly clambered down it and strolled out our side gate which I promptly closed.

With the Arch-Enemy gone, the coast looked clear for Patches to have one of her daily romps.

Things went calmly at first.

Patches inspected her inspecting places and spied a bird in a bush. Everything was quiet, so I stepped back inside to watch from our enclosed porch.

And then the Arch-Enemy returned.

As soon as I spotted the two cats in a stare off, I hurried outside. As I was bending over to grab Patches, Smokey bolted. The three of us were off to the races. Two blurs of fur raced around the yard – with me in futile pursuit – until Smokey wisely scrambled up and over our fence.

Patch skidded to a halt, pissed off that she had been foiled again from catching her Nemesis by the fence she could not climb and was too tall for her to jump.

I left her alone in the yard for a few minutes, letting her adrenaline taper off. She tends to bite anything in sight – including Laps and Cat Chow Bowl Filler-Uppers – immediately after having a run-in with her Arch-Enemy.

After a five-minute cool down, I brought her back inside for some Chow and a brushing.

Another December 25th.

Another Running of The Cats.

I hope it snows next Christmas.

Just Where Is THE Meth Capital?

Originally Posted Monday, August 31, 2009

The *Southeast Missourian* website recently ran a photo of a woman who looked very happy.

I thought this was odd since the picture was her booking photo from a drug bust. Shouldn't you look sad for a police mug shot or at least be unemotional? But this woman was smiling, appearing to be as happy as a lark.

I mentioned this to Matt, our online editor. He'd noticed the same thing.

"Are you surprised?" he asked me. "She was probably high when they took the photo."

And then he said The Phrase.

"They got her in Stoddard County. You know that's the Meth Capital of Missouri."

I've heard that phrase – something-or-other capital – thrown around a lot over the years. It seems that every city and town in the U.S. aspires to be the Capital of something. Even illicit narcotics are OK.

For instance, in Missouri we seem to have a lot of Meth Capitals. That's not surprising. Our state is often touted as the Meth Capital of the country. I don't know if that is true or not. That would then make lil' ol' Stoddard County the District of Columbia of Meth for the United States of America. That seems rather unlikely.

Personally, I think the whole Meth Capital issue is up for debate.

Just a week or so ago I read in the *St. Louis Post-Dispatch* that Jefferson County was The Meth Capital of Missouri. Stoddard County was not even mentioned in that article.

But here was the online editor of the *Southeast Missourian* telling me that Stoddard County was The Meth Capital of Missouri. Another newsroom editor chimed in that she thought Bollinger County was the Meth Capital of the Show Me State.

I guess it all depends on how you define what it takes to be labeled The Capital.

In the case of meth, perhaps you are the capital if your county's law enforcement has the most busts. Or perhaps the capital could be decided by the quantity of narcotics that are captured. One great big giant bust has to be more important than a dozen itsy-bitsy busts.

Or maybe the title of Meth Capital should take into account the entire population of a county when compared to the number of busts. If that were the case, I could see Stoddard County potentially being the Meth Capital of Missouri rather than Jefferson County. Jefferson County has nearly 220,000 residents, seven times more than Stoddard County.

Maybe we don't know where the REAL Meth Capital of Missouri actually is located, because those drug kingpins have managed to avoid detection. Jefferson and Stoddard Counties may just be contenders for the Meth-Dealers-Who-Have-Been-Stupid-Enough-To-Get-Caught Capital and some other county that has not had a single bust is in fact cranking out meth on an industrial scale. They could be the REAL Meth Capital and we wouldn't even know it.

This is a dilemma. How can the media know which county is or isn't the real Meth Capital of Missouri?

Tim from our design department was passing through the newsroom at the time of this discussion. He suggested we sponsor a "Meth-Off."

I like it. It's a good name. It's catchy. I like catchy.

Although I'm not really sure what it would take for a successful Meth-Off. Tim did not actually suggest any process for how you would exactly go about running one.

That seems to be a recurring problem here at *The Irony Of It All* blog. We're able to dream up outside-of-the-box solutions to problems or issues, but a lot of times we're a little sketchy on the exact process for actually accomplishing these Big Picture plans that we propose.

We're like The Capital of that kind of thing.

Hating My Bank

Originally Posted Thursday, September 10, 2009

I'm starting to hate my bank.

My wife and I use Bank of America and have for years. We've been with Centerre who was bought out by Boatmen's who was then bought out by NationsBank and finally by Bank of America. In short, we're pretty loyal customers.

I don't particularly want to hate my bank. Years ago, when I first opened my account, my bank had a number of local branches and ATMs, but thru the various mergers and acquisitions, they've been slowly whittling them away, like chairs being pulled during a cakewalk.

BofA is currently down to one branch in Cape Girardeau and – according to their website – two ATMs. I was shocked when I read that. BofA had another ATM besides the one at their lone branch on William?

The website directions and map to the second mystery ATM were a little vague, but I finally figured out that it is inside the mall, right in front of the main entrance. I never go in that way so that explains why I had no idea it was even there.

I know my wife and I could switch banks. There are numerous other financial institutions that we could consider who have as many – if not more – local branches and ATMs.

However, none are closer to my house than BofA and it would be a major hassle to relocate our loans. So, for the moment, I will resign myself to just complaining. Perhaps, the powers-that-be who make these decisions at BofA will someday get a clue, but I doubt if. I'm sure they don't live around here. Decisions of that kind likely originate from their headquarters in Charlotte, North Carolina.

To them, Cape is just another location on a great big spreadsheet with X number of accounts representing Y number of deposits and therefore only worthy of Z number of ATMs and branches. It's not personal, it's just business.

And while I understand the likely reasoning behind the branch and ATM attrition in our market, nobody says I have to like it. Frankly, BofA is starting to try my loyalty and patience. Sometimes you just don't have 20 minutes to wait in line at an ATM, and I loathe to use one of their competitor's machines and be slapped with a service fee.

It occurred to me that perhaps BofA is deliberately trying to annoy its customers so much that we will stop using their precious little ATMs. ATMs are an expense, you know. They're just like any complicated system, they break down and those repair guys are not cheap.

So it would be good for BofA's bottom line if less people used their ATMs and withdrew cash from their accounts by using their debit card at the grocery store. I guess that is what my wife and I are going to start doing. Whenever we check out at Schnucks or Wal-Mart, we'll get an extra twenty dollars.

Since, BofA is down to just one branch and two ATMs in the city, I think they should consider providing their customers with a little entertainment as we wile away our time waiting in the drive-thru line to use their services.

I think they should borrow the old advertising technique used by the Burma-Shave Company during the mid-twentieth century. Burma-Shave would have a series of 5 or 6 roadside signs that motorists could watch for as they were driving. Each sign related back to the previous one and they often rhymed.

Here are a couple of their roadside jingles from Wikipedia:

Your shaving brush / Has had its day / So why not / Shave the modern way / With / Burma-Shave

and

Shaving brushes / You'll soon see 'em / On the shelf / In some / Museum / Burma-Shave

Since this long-lived ad campaign was retired in 1963 when the Burma-Shave Company was sold to Phillip Morris, I figure that it's kind of up for grabs and that Bank Of America is free to use it wherever they have backed up drive-thrus and ATMs.

Here are a few suggestions they are free to use:

No one / Ever Said / An ATM / Meant / Faster Banking / BofA

I like that one, since it doesn't dance around the message and tells the customer that this is the way it is, so suck it up. Sometimes the customer just needs to be told that. However, I prefer the ones that rhyme. How about:

Need Some Cash? / This Is The Line / Just 10 More Minutes / You'll Be Just Fine / BofA

Or what do you think of:

Good News / And Give Thanks / While You've Been In This Line / We Bought Two More Banks / BofA

Or this one:

Customers Go / And Customers Come / You've Been In This Line / For An Hour? / Gee, You're Dumb. / BofA

Or my personal favorite:

Your House In Default? / Please Don't Pout / Maybe You Too / Can Get / A Federal Bailout / BofA

Note: The local branch of Bank of America mentioned in this blog added a second ATM a couple months after this essay originally appeared It made banking with them more tolerable.

Is It Wrong To Love My Trashcan?

Originally Posted Friday, September 18, 2009

I think I may love my trashcan.

At least I love one of my trashcans and not in the perverse way that you might find on a kinky website like TrashcanLust.com or DumpsterLuvin.net. No, I love it in a purely platonic, I-love-you-man, guy kind of way.

The trashcan is the one that I brought to my marriage. Ol' Blackie is what I call him, mainly because he's old and he's black.

My wife brought two trashcans to our marriage. I tolerate them since they are trashcans-in-law. One is called Bluey. He's blue. The other is named Wheel. He used to be named Wheels until an overly-aggressive refuse collection agent bounced him a little too hard on the sidewalk causing one of his two plastic tires to shatter. He's also missing a handle.

When he's full, you have to balance him just right to get him to roll on his lone wheel. It's kind of sad. Sort of like watching a 3-legged dog run after a stick tossed on an ice-covered pond.

The trashcans my wife and I bought a few years ago we call The Quads since there are four of them. I do not love The Quads. I don't even particularly like them. Frankly, The Quads have been great big disappointments. They are the cheapest waste receptacles I've ever owned.

I won't say who made those four, but the name sounds a little like Blubber Weighed. I thought when I bought The Quads that they were a good deal. They were a name-brand as far as plastic manufacturers go, made by the same company that made Bluey and they were reasonable-priced at about ten dollars each.

But holes quickly appeared in The Quad's soft, malleable plastic and within months of being acquired a couple of the cans had tears on their sides. One of the lids developed a bad split making it useless. I pitched it. The trashcans are still basically usable, but will they last 20 years like my trashcan or even my trashcans-in-law? Not in a heartbeat.

Currently, I use The Quads along with Ol' Blackie for primarily collecting and hauling yard waste to the local recycling center.

While Ol' Blackie has a couple of small holes in his bottom, he has no splits, his handles are rock-solid and his lid still fits great. Basically he is as sound as the day I bought him almost 20 years ago. Considering that he is just hard plastic and sits outside in the elements year-round, he is in remarkable shape.

Ol' Blackie has been a stalwart companion. He's carried tons of plaster and lathe and other assorted construction debris that comes with renovating several houses over the years. At times I've filled him with so much yard waste that I've had trouble just dragging him over to my truck for a trip to the recycling center. That might explain the holes on his bottom.

In a word, Ol' Blackie is reliable. And I'm sure he'll be there when the day comes that I need to put one or more of The Quads out of their misery and dispose of their rubbery remains by the curb.

After all, he is a trashcan's trashcan.

'Clunkers For Cruisers'

Originally Posted Friday, September 25, 2009

Before this week, there were two types of vehicles that I NEVER expected to be repossessed:

Trucks with full gun racks and police cars.

Basically, I believed they were repo-resistant for the same reason. The drivers of both vehicles are typically well-armed and not afraid to protect their property. I imagine those are the type of people that the typical repo-man does NOT want to deal with.

However, this belief – or at least half of it – was all shot to pieces earlier this week when five patrol cars for the Alexander County, Ill. Sheriff's Department were repossessed because the county defaulted on their payments.

Who knew you could repossess a police car? I certainly didn't.

However, the Alexander County Sheriff's Department did the right thing and turned their cruisers into the bank without an incident or involving a repo-man in their recovery.

It would have been an extremely awkward situation, if instead they had decided that protecting the citizenry of Alexander County was more important than repaying a measly little loan and had kept the cars in service to the public. Maybe that's how socialism starts.

Anyhow, I guess that just shows you the pecking order of bankers compared to law enforcement. Perhaps, the sheriff and his deputies will remember that the next time a bank robbery occurs in Alexander County.

"We'd like to come over there and chase down the thieves who held up the bank, but our Huffy police cruiser just threw a chain and it's going to be out of commission until we can afford to buy a new master link."

Really, this whole situation is quite sad for the citizens of Alexander County. Minutes after the story was released on the *Southeast Missourian* website, one reader quickly identified the cause of this problem as being the result of "Obama's economics."

The insinuation that Cairo and the rest of Alexander County were thriving under the Bush administration made me laugh. When exactly was the last time that the southern tip of Illinois could have been considered prosperous? Maybe 50 years ago when coal was still king in Southern Illinois?

I think that rather than point fingers and blame "The Other Guys" for this financial default in Alexander County, we should all pitch in and assist our fellow Americans.

For instance, the city of Cape Girardeau is holding it's annual surplus auction and among the goodies being sold are five older Ford Crown Victorias.

Wanna bet that they are ex-police cruisers? It's like fate. Alexander County needs five cruisers and Cape Girardeau County has five surplus cruisers. Perhaps the city could donate them to our Illinois neighbors as some kind of a tax-write off.

Or what about the back lots of all the local car dealerships that still have rows of those Cash for Clunkers trade-ins waiting to be trashed?

I propose we start a new program called Clunkers For Cruisers in which we take the best of these reputed wrecks and convert them into needed local law enforcement vehicles. We can just tell the feds that they were destroyed. They'll never find out. After all, who would think of checking a VIN number on an "Official Ford F-150 Police Cruiser?"

Now, some might say that a Ford F-150 – that model was one of the most popular traded in during the Cash for Clunkers program – is not a practical vehicle for law enforcement, but I disagree. I think it would be a very handy vehicle for patrolling the rough gravel back roads of Alexander County.

In addition, the sheriff and his deputies could use a rugged Ford F-150 and its sizable payload to haul a lot more prisoners around than they ever could with a Crown Vic.

And best of all, a Ford F-150 is ready-made for a gun-rack.

That makes them practically repo-resistant and that's important.

Dear Anal-Retentive Snow Plow Operator

Tuesday, February 3, 2009

Thank you for plowing my street. Perhaps, the next time, you can do it with your eyes open.

Yes, I know you are probably putting in a 12-hour shift or longer in an attempt to get the mess off the road. This winter storm has left behind precipitation that is as hard as concrete and extremely difficult to remove.

I know because I spent more than an hour shoveling the snow from my sidewalk and chiseling tire paths down the hill of my driveway so I too could go to work. I then spent another hour just getting my truck loose from its icy grip to the ground.

And when I got home from work last Thursday, I found that you had graded my street. Again, thank you.

I only minded a little that I had to shovel a 2-foot tall pile of snow and ice from in front of my driveway before I could even park. After all, the street had a nice clean path down the middle of it.

Again, I thank you.

But apparently, you are something of a perfectionist, because not 15 minutes after I finished removing the 2-foot tall pile and once again had a nice wide opening connecting my driveway to the street, you were back on my block scraping a little more.

So, before I could leave and go get some groceries, I had to shovel away another fresh pile of icy goodness blocking the mouth of my driveway.

This time I was not so happy.

Why did my street have to be visited by the only anal-retentive snowplow operator in the world?

How do I know you're anal-retentive? Because just a few minutes later you came down my street a third time, scraping just a little more. Thankfully, I had not left for the grocery store and was outside at that moment, so I managed to wave you away from my driveway before you pushed another pile in front of it.

I guess your eyes were open at that point since you didn't hit me.

Again, I thank you for plowing my street and for not hitting me.

But please remember that while you are putting in 12-hour shifts in a warm cab, behind the wheel of a powerful truck with a large blade, most homeowners don't have any power equipment capable of dealing with the ice and snow. We just have our shovels and our backs.

Perhaps, when you plow my street after the next snowstorm you can push the mess to the other side of the street rather than piling it up on mine that has 6 houses and usually several cars parked by the curb. The other side has only two houses and few cars ever park there. You may not know that, but hopefully you do now.

P.S. Just wanted to let you know that there were no vehicles parked in front of either house that uses my driveway. I know that is sometimes a justification for burying driveway entrances.

P.P.S. Again, thank you for plowing my street.

Is 'Stupid' a Pre-Existing Condition?

Originally Posted Thursday, October 08, 2009

I was waiting at a stoplight a couple weeks ago and noticed a fellow on a Harley. I neither "ride" nor usually pay any attention to bikers unless they've tinkered with their exhaust and go roaring by sounding like a Boeing 737 on take-off.

However, this guy's bike did not sound especially loud. No, what I noticed about him was his choice of footwear.

He was wearing flip-flops.

While I am a big proponent of personal freedom and believe that poor decisions by some of my fellow human beings are <u>not</u> meant to be legislated away and are actually God's way of thinning the Homo sapien herd, I felt compelled to pull this guy over and ask him what his plans were if he happened to wipe out his bike and lived. His choice of flip-flops pretty much guaranteed he would wind up with severely mangled feet if he did have an accident, requiring significant medical care.

Basically, I wanted to know if he had health insurance and if he did, did that policy consider "stupid" a pre-existing condition?

And more importantly, would he sign a waiver guaranteeing that the cost of my own medical care would not increase because of my fellow citizen's choice at exercising his personal freedom.

I look at it this way:

Why should I pay for someone else being stupid?

I think the same thing about all these people riding scooters around town, zipping along at 20 plus miles per hour without any head protection. I know a helmet doesn't necessarily look cool and could really muss their hair, but what happens if they wipe out and suffer a brain injury? Who is going to pay for the care they will need for the rest of their life?

I don't think it should be me. Why should I pay for them being stupid?

Unfortunately, stupidity is such a rampant disease in this country that I think the CDC should get involved.

For instance, I saw on TV the other evening a clip of what looked like a teenager attempting a stunt with his skateboard. If you've ever been videotaped on a skateboard and the footage gets aired on a TV show, it is never a good sign.

In this case, the wannabe stunt boy wiped out going down a hill and the only thing that stopped him was his privates and an electric-pole guy wire.

I'll give you a second to reflect on that and all the men to recover...

While I don't know what exactly became of this particular junior stuntman – or the legions of other Johnny Knoxville impersonators you see on caught-on-video clip shows trying incredibly stupid feats of derring-do – one can only assume that a hospital emergency room had to be somewhere in his immediate plans following this wipeout.

Perhaps, he had insurance, but just as likely not. And who pays for his medical needs resulting from this idiocy? It's likely that we all do. That's the reason that a Tylenol costs $40 when given to us by a nurse during a hospital stay. The pill and the paper cup it comes in costs a nickel and the other $39.95 goes towards paying off "charitable" hospital expenses incurred by risk-takers like this fellow who bet and lost with no way to pay the medical bills they've racked up.

Again, why should I pay for them being stupid?

Besides the day or two after I was born, I've never been hospitalized and I've only had to go to an emergency room four times in my life. I credit my track record to basically being a cautious individual. I buckle my seat belt. I wear a helmet when I ride a bicycle. And I make sure never to start a sentence with the phrase "Hey guys, watch this."

That's how I've managed to survive essentially unscathed to the old age of 42.

However, I don't believe that anyone should use me as a role model. You should be your own person. Do your own thing. If you want to ride your Harley wearing flip-flops or your scooter with no helmet, you go right ahead. If you fancy yourself a skateboard-stud and wish to mimic tricks you've seen on TV, that is your prerogative.

But if you wipe out and turn yourself into a vegetable because you exercised your right to do whatever you damn well please and it turned out badly, then I don't believe that myself or any other citizen should have to foot the bill for your medical care.

After all, why should we pay for stupid?

Lost Pet. Brown With Curly Hair. Weighs One Ton.

Originally Posted Wednesday, October 14, 2009

I'm a bit of a newspaper junkie. Whenever I travel I always pick up the local paper to see a different perspective on the world.

While big city newspapers – or "metros" as they are often called – are interesting, I especially enjoy reading small-town weeklies. Local news dominates in these publications and state or national issues are rarely mentioned.

Instead, they cover their market's minutiae, all the births and deaths, and trials and tribulations of the average people who are their readers. They also report on the occasional oddball local story – like a tomato that resembles Abraham Lincoln – that would not be considered "newsworthy" for a daily publication.

My hometown weekly paper had one of these obscure tales buried on page seven of a recent issue. However, this particular story had nothing to do with produce.

No, it was about a lost family pet. There's nothing strange about that, right? After all, pets wander off everyday.

Except in this case, the pet was a buffalo.

The buffalo broke out of its pen and though the owners tried to find it – they even used a helicopter in an effort to spot the burly beast – they were unsuccessful. Finally, they recruited a hunter who tracked the buffalo down. It had wandered several miles and must have been intent on making it back to the Great Plains. The hunter put it down with 3 shots.

Now, before you get too weepy-eyed that a sadistic hunter shot somebody's poor little pet, please keep in mind that this pet was a buffalo. Buffalo are not only big, they can be pretty ill-tempered and you don't want to spook them. Having one as a "pet" is a little comparable to having "Snuffles" the alligator or "Fluffy" the tiger greet you when you come home from work every evening.

Besides the fact that a buffalo was involved in this incident – I'm pretty sure it would not make the Top 100 Most Common Pets List – the other thing that piqued my interest was the last sentence of the story:

But even this feat (of tracking down and shooting this buffalo) proved to be no challenge for (the) avid hunter who was also reported to have killed a deer with a pocketknife last season.

That is worth repeating. The hunter who tracked down this buffalo had <u>reportedly</u> killed a deer with a pocketknife.

A couple years ago, I hit a 12-point buck in Kentucky with an SUV going 35 miles an hour. The collision caused $7000 in damage to my vehicle. That deer not only got up, but I swear it stuck its tongue out at me before running off as if nothing had happened.

With that personal experience in mind, I'm supposed to believe that this hunter managed to kill a deer with a pocketknife, a feat that I was unable to accomplish with a 2-ton SUV?

OK, I suppose it is possible. Perhaps the deer was sleeping when the hunter came upon it. Thinking fast, he pulled out his Swiss Army Knife and mortally wounded it.

Or maybe he lay in wait, crouched up in a tree stand until an unsuspecting Bambi came strolling by and pounced on it with knife in hand.

Or the more likely truth is that he'd already wounded the deer with his rifle and he finished it off with his hunting knife. Perhaps that is the real story and it has gotten exaggerated over time with the deer getting bigger and bigger and the knife getting smaller and smaller.

Give it a couple years and I bet the deer in this story will have become a moose with rabies that cornered the hunter in a cave and the only weapon he had on his person to fight his way out was one of those file thingies that flip out of toenail clippers.

That would make for a great story. And I look forward to reading about it in my hometown weekly newspaper.

An Outhouse With A Bad Mullet

Originally Posted Wednesday, October 28, 2009

Halloween reminds me of outhouses.

Not those plastic Porta-Potties that you see lined up at events like county fairs or outdoor festivals, but rather those simple wooden sheds that often had the silhouette of a half-moon cut into the door.

While Halloween and outhouses might be a strange association to some – OK, probably to most – allow me to elaborate.

As a child, my elementary school was located on Highway 61 just north of the bustling metropolis of Bloomsdale, Missouri in northern Ste. Genevieve County.

At that time Bloomsdale had a Bi-Rite, a hardware store, a church, two gas stations and a couple of bars including the Dew Drop Inn. There were no stoplights in metropolitan Bloomsdale just a flashing yellow warning light where Mill Hill Road teed into Highway 61.

It was at this intersection that a giant pile of junk magically appeared on the morning of November first, the year I was in first-grade.

While the event may not have been a magical occurrence to the grown-ups who had to clean up the mess, it was to me, six-years-old and oblivious to the stupidity adults could talk themselves into after drinking excess quantities of alcoholic beverages.

But from my perspective, there was something incredibly cool about riding the bus to school that foggy November morning and seeing a mountain of junk appear out of the mist in the middle of the road. It was like spotting Big Foot or seeing a ghost.

This debris was apparently gathered from behind the various local businesses with most being dragged from the collection located in the back lot of the ironically named Speed's Service Station.

Speed was quite a nice fellow, but his business was no Jiffy Lube. You didn't get a 10-minute oil change at his station. You either left your vehicle there and went next door to the Dew Drop Inn for a cold Coke and to listen to the old-timers complain about what was wrong with the world, or you walked over to the hardware store to browse its aisles.

I never heard who was actually responsible for assembling this giant pile of junk on Halloween night. Presumably, it was some of the evening regulars from the Dew Drop Inn who thought it was a fun "trick" to play after they had downed a few beers.

While the assortment of junk in the middle of the road was an awesome sight to a six-year-old, the oddest item of the entire collection had to be the old wooden outhouse.

I'm not sure if the outhouse was a part of the junkyard behind Speed's or if the tricksters scrounged it up from one of the other nearby properties, but it loomed above the collection of old tires and rusty car doors like some kind of refuse royalty.

While the location of this particular outhouse was both odd and funny to me, I was not unfamiliar with outdoor privies. At the time, my parent's farm still had one.

It was a weathered single-seater outhouse with the traditional half-moon cut into the door and a well-fed honeysuckle vine growing up and over the top of it like a mullet gone bad.

Oh sure, we had regular indoor plumbing in our home, but this privy was a lingering monument to an age of human-waste collection from days gone by that my dad had not yet gotten around to razing.

Eventually, he did just that, hacking the honeysuckle vine to pieces and dismembering the building board by board. He hauled those remains to the edge of our property and dumped them into a bottomless sinkhole that was the resting place for countless loads of castoffs from the farm.

And you would think that would be the end of that story, wouldn't you? But it's not.

While the Halloween shenanigans of the evening regulars at the Dew Drop Inn stopped by the time I was in the third grade, and Speed cleared out the mess from behind his station so there was no junk that could be appropriated for mischief, reports of strange, unexplained sightings began circulating between neighbors in northern Ste. Genevieve County.

Even to this day the stories persist.

It is said that on moonless autumn nights when the air is crisp and dense fog has rolled off of the meandering Establishment Creek, that the mist will sometimes part as you're rounding a blind-curve on some back road around Bloomsdale and a hulking Cyclops will appear, squatting in front of you squinting with its glowing eye.

As you slam on your brakes and fishtail on the loose gravel, the image of It – whatever It is – will linger for a second or two, before disappearing into the swirling mist.

You'll rub your eyes and think you're just imagining things. Maybe It was a big buck or It was the result of one beer too many at the Dew Drop Inn. Or perhaps It was just the fog playing tricks with your mind and with the lights of your highbeams.

But a little part of you will know the truth and you won't be able to forget what you really saw.

It was a weathered outhouse sporting a bad mullet.

Smoking Bans Don't Go Far Enough

Originally Posted Friday, November 13, 2009

I was leaving work at lunch one day this past week and smelled slightly overdone microwave popcorn presumably coming from the company break room. I wrinkled my nose and quickly left the building because this odor offended my selectively-delicate nostrils.

I use the phrase "selectively-delicate" for a reason.

Having grown up "in the country" some odors that I don't even notice make others wretch. For instance, I once helped clean out a silo whose bottom was full of fermenting silage. A co-worker on the job couldn't stomach the stench of the sickeningly sweet-smelling substance, but it didn't bother me.

And I'm also not phased by the pungent odors you will find lingering around commercial swine operations. I've been told that fragrance can make a person swear off bacon for life. Or at least for breakfast.

While some smells don't bother me in the least, others make me gag.

Such as burnt, microwave popcorn.

I'm also not too fond of burning leaves or the people who feel they must torch them. I think that's an asinine and completely unnecessary process that stinks up an entire neighborhood on a pleasant fall day and is only beneficial to the closet-pyromaniac who started the blaze. Can you tell I really hate burning leaves? Even the smallest fire can be smelled blocks away hours after it has been put out.

I'm also not especially fond of cigarette or cigar smoke, but I have devised an ingenious solution to that problem:

If a smoker is smoking close by and the smoke is bothering me, I move.

That's pretty radical thinking, right? Sometimes I take just a step back, sometimes more, three at the most. That gets the job done for me.

There are folks that have a significantly more extreme solution than mine and believe that smoking and smokers are the epitome of wickedness and should be banned everywhere on the planet and possibly even on the moon.

However, the moon ban is still being debated amongst that coalition and they may make it the "designated smoking section" for any earthlings still wishing to "light up" just to show that they do have a modicum of tolerance.

Some people from this coalition might sneer at my solution – move away – as being too simplistic for avoiding smokers. They might point out that the poor waitress or waiter at a restaurant can't move away from any smoking customers because that is their job. Here's my solution to those restaurant workers who can't stomach the customers who choose to smoke:

Quit.

If the restaurant they are employed at allowed smoking before they were hired then they should have known that there was a risk of encountering smoke while at work. It was an existing "danger" inherent with the job.

Some jobs have innate risk.

For instance, I've never once considered applying for a job as a lifeguard because there is an inherent danger of drowning and since I can't swim, that makes it doubly so.

But based on the same logic of some members of the smoking-ban coalition, IF I choose to apply for a lifeguard position and IF I was actually hired for that job despite my one itsy-bitsy flaw – you know, the whole I-can't-swim issue – THEN I could request that everyone stay out of the pool since it posed an inherent danger to me as the lifeguard. I suppose sunbathing would be OK.

Recently, the city of St. Louis and St. Louis County voted to outlaw smoking in public places and Illinois has had a ban for the entire state for nearly two years. Apparently, this upsurge in anti-smoking legislation is encouraging campaigns elsewhere including here in Cape Girardeau.

Whether or not the local movement gets enough traction to put the issue up for a public vote is questionable. Personally, it makes no difference to me since I've already devised the aforementioned and practically foolproof system to avoid smokers whose habit bothers me.

But if the local anti-smoking committee broadens their thinking beyond just tobacco products, I might be convinced to vote in favor of a ban.

After all, burning leaves and charred microwave popcorn does offend my selectively-delicate nostrils.

But please don't think I'm such an intolerant S.O.B. who would want to universally ban the burning of leaves and the charring of popcorn.

Hardly. I would gladly allow any persons who wished to pursue those interests to do so at the same location as the soon-to-be-announced "designated smoking section."

You know, the one on the moon.

The 'Fighting Smileys' of Wal-Mart U.

Originally Posted Friday, November 20, 2009

I have believed for years that competition was a good thing.

After all, I've been a good little consumer my whole life and I was taught at an early age that competition amongst businesses was one of the key components to a successful and robust capitalistic society.

Monopolies were bad, I was told. That's why the federal government broke up Ma Bell in the early 1980s, to foster competition. That's also why many consumers like me were happy whenever Wal-Mart decided to open a store near our homes. They were and are strong competitors and prices all over the area would drop when Sam Walton's discount chain goose-stepped into town.

I realize a lot of mom-and-pop stores and lesser-aggressive national retailers closed after Wal-Mart marched into a market. They either couldn't or wouldn't compete and closing was the price they paid. That's the sometimes seedier side of capitalism. And while the competition was bad for some of the existing retailers, it was good for the local consumers.

That's why I was amazed when I read an article in a recent *Southeast Missourian* discussing the latest developments from the Cape Girardeau area community college coalition.

Southeast Missouri State University and Three Rivers Community College are attempting to work out an arrangement so those two institutions can jointly-run a community college here in Cape.

It amazes me that they're trying to bury the proverbial hatchet and not in each other. There's been a lot of bad blood between those two institutions. But that wasn't the part of the story that really blew me away.

What amazed me most was the fact that the president of the Cape Girardeau Area Chamber of Commerce reportedly *"encouraged the group to support the arrangement between Southeast and Three Rivers, saying it will keep other competitors out of the area."*

Talk about changing my consumeristic world-view! Black is no longer black! White is no longer white! Chartreuse is no longer... whatever color chartreuse was to begin with!

I've believed my whole life that competition was good, but now the well-respected president of our local Chamber of Commerce is essentially saying that competition is bad, that choice is a not a good thing. How can that be?

But then, after I found a paper bag to stick over my head and finally quit hyper-ventilating – drastic changes in my world-view tends to do that to me – I gave the matter some thought.

This declaration by the president of our local Chamber of Commerce actually made sense. His job is to be the advocate of businesses that are already in the area, not businesses that <u>might</u> want to come into the area.

Local businesses like Southeast Missouri State University which are dues paying members to the local Chamber of Commerce deserve that organization's protection against any unwanted outsiders.

So I applaud the President of the Chamber for taking the stand against any higher education interlopers who might want to even consider weaseling their way into our market.

You stay away, you University of Phoenixes and you ITTs and you other educational options! We don't need you here in Cape Girardeau and we don't want you here, cherry-picking the higher educational-variation of our low-hanging fruit.

If anybody is going to teach our college freshmen English and math skills they should have mastered by the time they were in the eighth grade, it should be somebody local, not some outsider trying to shoe-horn their way into our market!

However, if one of our existing local businesses wants to expand their "product-line" and get into the lucrative business of higher-education, I suppose that's a whole other matter. That kind of competition is OK. It's "friendly" <u>local</u> competition. We like local.

For instance, it would be OK if a business such as the Wal-Mart on Seimers Drive decided to start issuing degrees.

Wal-Mart College – Wal-lege they could call it, since that sounds more folksy and a lot less pretentious than Wal-Mart University – even has a ready-made mascot in the form of the smiley-face logo that they used for years.

It doesn't matter that Wal-Mart quit using the smiley-face in 2006. It would make a great school mascot for Wal-lege. I bet the Fightin' Smileys football team will kick butt both on <u>and</u> off the field.

You want a beer while tailgating? Forget about $7 for a draft. It's only $6.93 at the Wal-lege concession stand!

Oh sure, the world's largest retailer may not be qualified to churn out Physics or Music majors, but how about Agribusiness (lawn and garden department) or Applied Mathematics & Statistics *(any cashier position)* or Behavior Disorders (You ever been to Wal-Mart on a Friday or Saturday night? It's literally a Petri dish of people with behavior disorders).

Wal-lege can also guarantee that every class has 100% hands-on experiential learning. I've heard that's a plus. And if you play your cards right, and come to class everyday, Wal-Mart just might offer you an honest-to-goodness job after you have earned your degree.

Welcome To The Bank Of Brad

Originally Posted Wednesday, November 26, 2008

I've decided to start a bank.

I made this decision after noticing that the feds appear to be shoveling piles of money at any bank that strolls by in a short skirt with bad assets. Even businesses that you would not traditionally consider to be banks such as American Express and GMAC are applying to become banks or bank-holding companies. All so they can qualify for their shovel-full of cash.

At this rate, it's only a matter of time until we see the First National Bank of Waffle House.

"Would you like free checking with your French toast?"

This is why I've decided to start my own bank. The Bank of Brad or BOB for short. It practically writes it's own marketing campaign.

"Don't invest with the rest. Go with who you know. Trust your money with BOB."

Catchy, isn't it? I even have a logo.

Of course, the point of all this hard work - that slogan and logo took <u>almost</u> <u>15 minutes</u> to create – is not to actually get any depositors.

Heck, if I had depositors that would mean I would have to have tellers and ATMs and maybe even a building that looked bank-like. And I'd probably need a website and certainly a more extensive marketing plan than my current logo and slogan.

Frankly, that is way more time and energy than I want to invest. To be honest, I don't want to have any customers. Customers require customer service, and that is not my forte.

Now, it does seem that the possession of "toxic assets" may be a requirement for some of this fed cash. The simple definition of a "toxic asset" is a risky, high yield investment that has gone south.

Basically, the banks made large bets, and the dealer hit blackjack. They gambled. They lost. Now they want help from the feds.

Kind of sounds like loaner remorse to me.

While I've never had loaner remorse, I certainly have had buyers remorse.

Haven't we all? We've all bought something that in hindsight was not such a good idea.

Before I was married, I bought a little row house in south St. Louis and put about $7000 into it. Then I moved to Cape Girardeau. It took 2 years to sell and sold for what I originally paid for it before the improvements. Can you say, "location, location, location?" Bye-bye seven grand.

It was definitely a toxic asset to me and by marriage, my wife.

But that was then and this is now. Perhaps the fact I once owned a "toxic asset" will be enough to qualify me, uh I mean BOB – the financial institution that I control – for a nice big handout from the feds.

After all, I have a logo and a slogan.

I'll even bring my own shovel.

'**G****** Zhu Zhu Robotic Hamsters**'

Originally Posted Wednesday, December 02, 2009

It was an image seen thousands of times during the worst financial crisis since the Great Depression.

A dirty figure leaning against a light post, a cardboard sign propped up in front of him. The scrawl on it indicated he wanted a job.

But this wasn't a scene from St. Louis or some other large city, but here in Cape Girardeau out by I-55 and Route K. I don't know if I'd ever seen a sadder-looking fellow. He didn't even attempt to wave down any passing motorists, letting the sign do all the work. Between his lips he gripped the nub of a smoldering cigarette that a smoker had discarded while waiting for the light to change.

It's not usually in my nature to stop when I see characters like this one, but something about him made me. He was... different. I pulled over, got out of my truck and asked him his name.

He said it was Harold.

"Harold what?" I asked.

"Just Harold," he replied as he took one last long drag on the cigarette before flicking it away.

"So what's your story, Harold? How'd you get here? How'd you get like this?"

He looked kind of pissed.

"How'd I get here? I thumbed a ride with a semi hauling cheap Chinese crap to your Wal-Mart, that's how I got here. Now, if you are really interested in my story, I'm kind of parched," he said, smacking his lips.

By coincidence, I'd just been to the Wal-Mart that had gotten the load of "cheap Chinese crap" and had a bottle of tequila in my truck. He chugged half of its contents before wiping his lips with his extraordinarily hairy forearm. He belched and asked me if I had any cigarettes. When I told him I didn't smoke, he shuffled over to the curb where he found a fresh butt. He returned to his spot against the light post.

"Now where were we? Oh yeah, how did I get like this, begging for work at an intersection in Southeast Missouri?"

He took a drag.

"I had a good job up to a few weeks ago down south. I'd worked there all of my life. Lived there, too. Then one day, out of the blue, the owners told me my services were no longer needed, that I was being let go. I found out from my co-worker Spike, that they were replacing me with some robotic junk made in China."

"Did they let Spike go?"

"Naw. Spike is in security. I think folks in security are pretty safe from this recession."

"So did the owners give you any severance pay?"

"Sort of. They let me keep my tools. You know the plastic tubes I'd run through to entertain their stupid kids and the wheel I'd jog on for exercise. They said the robots didn't need those. They had their own equipment.

"A lot of good the severance did me. I've already lost most of it. I got into a poker game with some guinea pigs and they took me to the f****** cleaners. All I have left is that travel ball." He waved his paw at the clear plastic sphere sitting in the grass a few feet away.

"I even tried getting a job as a gerbil, but they said I was too big and had no tail. I don't think my life can get any worse. And it's all because of those G****** Zhu Zhu robotic hamsters."

"I've heard of them, Harold. They're supposed to be the hot toy this year. I read that the company that makes them is based in St. Louis. Are many of your friends losing their jobs because of the Zhu Zhus?"

"Hell, yes! I know a half-dozen that all got pink slips at the same time as me. They say they might sell millions of them. Millions! Can you believe it? What are all of the out-of-work hamsters like me going to do? It's not like we've got a huge-skill set."

Harold got a hard-look on his face and took a long drag on the cigarette nub.

"Those SOBs have got to be stopped! Stopped for the good of pet kind, I tell you! This year it's hamsters, but what about next year? Robotic gerbils or guinea pigs. God help us if they starting making cats or dogs. No, those SOBs have got to be stopped and stopped NOW. Didn't you say the company that makes those little pieces of s*** is out of St. Louis?"

"Yeah. I think the company is called Cepia."

"Cepia... well those b******* shouldn't have messed with this hamster. They have no idea what I am capable of."

Harold the Hamster appeared to have a new lease on life.

Gone was the dejected soul, leaning against the light post. Before me was a rodent with a mission, a renewed sense of purpose.

He tossed what was left of the bottle of tequila into the travel ball and squeezed in along side it. And without another word he headed north on the interstate with only one thing obviously on his mind.

Payback.

The Bogey-Committee

Originally Posted Friday, December 04, 2009

As I've gotten older, I've come to dislike crowds more and more.

That's why my butt was nice and toasty under a blanket in my bed in the wee hours of Black Friday rather than standing in a line outside some store waiting for it to open up so I could take advantage of one of their Super-Duper, Never-Before-Seen-And-Never-To-Be-Seen-Again Deals in the pre-dawn hours on the day after Thanksgiving.

I just don't need or want anything that bad to fight those crowds.

Besides crowds, I'm also not too nuts about children squawling in public. I know I may have squawled a time or two growing up and perhaps my memory is fooling me, but I don't recall children being quite as loud and obnoxious out in public when I was child in the 1970's.

I guess it might be because parents' back then thought nothing of "disciplining" an overly vocal child. And unless you were particularly stupid or particularly whiny, you quickly learned that the only thing that squawling got you was a tender tooshy or the promise of one when you got home.

But that was then. Today any parent who even considers disciplining their child in public has to consider the fact that some do-gooder might turn them into social services for "child abuse."

Now, before I go any further, I want to be clear about one thing:

I am NOT suggesting that people beat their children. Beating your own children is a bad thing. I believe that most parents cannot assess a potential discipline situation dispassionately without letting other things affect their judgment such as the fact that two weeks before little Jimmy left his bicycle laying in the driveway behind their brand-new car and they drove over it.

So I repeat, it is a bad thing for parents to beat their own children.

But I do think it would be beneficial to society as a whole if we let total strangers beat your children when they were misbehaving in public.

Perhaps, children wouldn't turn into obnoxious terrors out in the community if they knew that a complete stranger might come striding out of the crowd to squelch their squawling. You know, kind of like the Bogey-Man who lurked under my bed growing up.

However, I realize that we live in a democratic society and to have a Bogey-Man who is judge, jury and the figurative executioner would just not be applicable for ultra politically correct 21st century America.

However, I think a "Bogey-Committee" would be appropriate.

The Bogey-Committee would be made up of adults, none of which actually applied to be a member of the Bogey-Committee. That would be part of the screening processes. If you want to be on the Bogey-Committee, then that might indicate you

110   Typos & Awl

actually like to beat children so therefore you <u>can't</u> be on the committee. It would be a lot like jury duty.

Here's how the Bogey-Committee would work:

Let's say that on the Tuesday prior to Thanksgiving, you needed a couple items from the local grocery store. However, knowing that the grocery store would likely be jam-packed – since it was the Tuesday before Thanksgiving <u>and</u> you really hate crowds – you go there about 9:30 pm.

That's a smart move on your part because the store is nearly empty and quite pleasant <u>except</u> for a squawling four-year old who can be heard all the way from the vegetables to the magazines. The child is quite unhappy and is apparently determined to make everyone else in the store just as unhappy as he. He won't shut up.

However, unbeknownst to the squawling child, you've been selected to be a member of the Bogey-Committee whose mission is to democratically decide whether a child should be disciplined for being a royal brat in public.

So you – as a member of the Bogey-Committee – would yell out "I call a meeting of the Bogey-Committee!"

As long as two other Bogey-Committee members were present in the store – the B.C. is partially modeled after the 3-person County Commission system – a decision would quickly be made regarding the fate of the squawling child.

In this case, that decision would be a paddling and you would stride up to the screaming rug-rat, squat down to his level and say to him, "Son, I'm with the Bogey Committee."

Now as long as his parents have done their job of indoctrinating him – *"You better be a good boy in public or the Bogey-Committee will get you!"* – that simple seven-word sentence would probably be the end of the entire incident.

The child would be scared witless and would immediately quit squawling, which is all that the Bogey-Committee really wants to accomplish. No paddling would actually have to take place. No one on the Committee wants to beat children. They just want the children to behave themselves in public and if that requires scaring the dickens out of them, then so be it.

Personally, I think this is a fine solution for this problem.

And to get the ball rolling, I will be the first person to volunteer <u>not</u> to be a member of the committee.

Things I have in common with the Tasmanian Devil

Originally Posted Thursday, December 4, 2008

In my office at work I have several items featuring the likeness of the Tasmanian Devil of Warner Brothers cartoon fame.

There's a ceramic note dispenser, a battery-powered pencil sharpener and several figurines. At home I have a maquette which features Taz in 3 common poses. Animators use maquettes to help them draw characters.

I'm not sure why I like these trinkets so much. Well they are kind of kitschy, and I do like kitschy. In a goofy way, Taz reminds me of, well, me.

I have a couple things in common with Taz.

We both growl a lot. Him because he is a Tazmanian Devil and according to the Zoology Department at Warner Brothers that's what Tasmanian Devils do. I growl a lot because of my occupation.

Snowballs and other stuff tend to roll downhill and while the information technology department may not be at the very bottom of that hill, we're darn close. Everything in a newspaper is connected to a computer and when things go wrong, my department often gets the call to get things right.

And when you've been doing that kind of work for over 15 years, you have a tendency to growl.

I also have an under-bite just like Taz. I didn't realize I had an under-bite until several years ago when I broke a tooth on a wayward piece of bone in a chicken pot pie at a Cracker Barrel. The dentist I went to told me that:

(1) I needed a crown to replace the mangled tooth. *Ka-Ching!*

(2) I had an under-bite and he could easily fix it by breaking my jaw and rewiring it. *Ouch! Ka-Ching! Ouch! Ka-Ching! Ouch! Ka-Ching!*

He told me that some people with under-bites have severe headaches. Considering that I never have headaches, I respectively declined his offer and allowed him to fit me with a crown.

Needless to say, I started going to another dentist after that.

Why I've Never Been A Cow

Originally Posted Monday, December 15, 2008

I'm not sure if reincarnation exists, but if it does, I'm pretty sure I've never been a cow in some past life.

I love my leather coats too much.

I never had a leather coat growing up. Wal-Mart and Sears didn't sell them back then.

But then I went to college and one day I stopped at an army surplus / pawn shop that was located in downtown Cape Girardeau at the corner of Broadway and Spanish. It's a lot now.

They had an old used motorcycle jacket that was in great shape. It was love at first sight. It didn't matter that I didn't have a motorcycle or had any interest in buying a motorcycle or even riding a motorcycle.

But I know that if I did have a motorcycle and happened to wipe out, I would want to be wearing that jacket. It's a beast, weighing over 9 pounds. I'm not sure what cow it came from, but I imagine it was old bull with a bad disposition.

I love that jacket. It still creaks when I wear it, even after 20 years.

Not long after acquiring that jacket, I saw some faux bomber jackets at a store in West Park Mall.

These were patterned after jackets worn by aviators in World War II complete with "authentic" bomber patches. I had to have one. I guess they did a good job on them since a gentleman once asked me if I'd gotten the jacket from my grandfather.

And so my leather jacket collection grew. I got a couple more bombers. My wife bought me a nice black one for Christmas one year. I got another one for my 15th anniversary at work.

I'm up to about 6 or 7. I think I have enough for now.

Maybe in my next life, I will be reincarnated as a bottle of saddle soap and a nice shammy.

It would be appropriate.

The Adolf Hitler Campbell Trilogy – Part 1

Originally Posted Thursday, December 18, 2008

There was a story in the news this week about a New Jersey couple who were trying to get their 3-year-old son's full name put on a birthday cake and the grocery store refused.

The child's name? Adolf Hitler Campbell.

Do we need any further proof that there should be some kind of test before people can be allowed to have a child?

Some people – and I think the parents of this boy would qualify – apparently give more thought into buying a flat-screen TV than they do over naming their own kids. I can only imagine how this naming choice came about...

March 2005: The future "parents" in the Wal-Mart electronics department.

He: *This is a mighty tough decision. Should we go with the LCD or the plasma TV?*

She: *Well I like the 50-inch one, over there. It's got a good picture.*

He: *I like it too honey, but I don't know if we have room for it in the double-wide.*

She: *If you moved the Kegerator you'd have room.*

He: *If I told you once, I told you at least a dozen time, I am not moving the Kegerator. I can't watch football without my Kegerator. I'll move it, as soon as you move the karaoke machine.*

She: *The karaoke machine has to be in the living room, you know that.*

He: *Yeah, I know. You like to watch Celine Dion while you sing along. You might as well forget it, honey. You are never gonna get on American Idol.*

She: *Well, at least I have dream.*

He: *I do too have a dream! And one of these days my system for playing PowerBall is going to payoff big time and then you're gonna be sorry you said that. Anyhow, enough arguing. This TV purchase is too important. I think I know what will work. Why don't we sit the plasma TV on top of the Kegerator? We can lean it up against the wall. That way I don't need to move the Kegerator and we don't have to spend money on some expensive mounting bracket.*

She: *Oh honey, you're just so smart! And I know your Powerball system is going to hit one of these days. You know, getting a new TV and all is making me feel kind of frisky. Let's go home and make another baby.*

He: *Don't have to ask me twice. Let's get the TV and go. Say, if it's a boy baby, let's name him Adolf Hitler.*

She: *Well, if it's a girl I want to name her Celine. Who's Adolf Hitler?*

He: *I dunno. Some guy I saw on a war show on the History Channel. He had a cool mustache.*

The Adolf Hitler Campbell Trilogy – Part 2

Originally Posted Monday, January 5, 2009

Fair warning.

This is another blog about the kid whose parents named him after Adolf Hitler. I know I'm repeating a topic, but I look at it this way.

If CNN host Nancy Grace can talk non-stop, 24 hours a day, 7 days a week for months on end about Caylee Anthony – the Florida child who disappeared late last spring whose body was just discovered in mid-December – without ever *once* catching a breath, I can at least run another blog on Adolf Hitler Campbell.

Who knows. Maybe I will even write a third to make a trilogy.

It could be kind of like *The Lord of The Rings*, but without hobbits. There are definitely orcs though. Some people might call them the parents of poor little Adolf.

For those of you, not familiar with either the previous blog or the news story upon which it was based, some "parents" in New Jersey wanted their son's full name – Adolf Hitler Campbell – put on his third birthday cake. When one grocery store refused, it became news.

Previously, I tried to contemplate how on God's green earth, these "parents" could have possibly decided that naming their child after the most infamous man in the 20th century was a good idea.

In this episode of *As the Dumbasses Spawn*, Father Orc gets a call from lil' Adolf's Day Care Center:

Tracy, the Daycare Manager: *Hello Mr. Campbell. This is Tracy from day care. We're having another problem with Adolf.*

Father Orc: *What did he do this time? Is he picking on that Steinberg kid again?*

Tracy: *No, not this time. Today he wouldn't let any of the other children play in the sandbox during play period. He kept yelling "Mein Sandkasten" and goose-stepping around it.*

Father Orc: *So, what's the big deal about that? If he called dibs, then the sandbox should be his.*

Tracy: *Sir, we don't encourage children to "call dibs." We encourage children to share.*

Momma Orc (breaking into the conversation): *Hello, did I hear Cher mentioned? I love Cher. I could karaoke to her practically all night long.*

Father Orc: *Darlene, will you get off the other phone. We are not talking about Cher. We're talking about SHAR-ring. The day care says Adolf is piggin' up the sandbox.*

Tracy: *Sir, we seem to have another problem. Adolf is starting to show other aggressiveness while playing.*

Father Orc: *How so?*

Tracy: *Well, he likes to organize his Matchbox cars into columns and rows with his dinosaur at the front, and when the other kids step away from their toys, he uses the T-Rex to bash their toys to pieces.*

Father Orc: *Yeah, he likes to play war. Ain't it cute?*

Tracy: *No sir, it is not cute. It's actually a little disturbing.*

Father Orc: *Hold it a second. Our little one is getting' into something.* (yelling away from the phone) *Josef! Josef Stalin Campbell! You get your butt away from that Kegerator! Darlene! Come get Josef! He's trying to stick a Pop Tart in the Blue Ray player!* (back to the phone) *Sorry about that. We just got that player for Christmas. I'll tell ya, our little one's a really stinker. Some might say he makes Adolf look like a saint.*

The Adolf Hitler Campbell Trilogy – Part 3

Originally Posted Wednesday, January 21, 2009

Three New Jersey children with Nazi-inspired names have been placed in the custody of that state. The reason for the intervention has not been released to the public and probably won't be since they are minors.

Contrary to a dastardly rumor being spread on the Internet, this blog had nothing – I repeat, nothing – to do with this act of sanity by the state of New Jersey.

Ok, so I exaggerated a little. There was no rumor started on the Internet and if there was, I probably would have been the one to start it. Hey, you do what you have to do to generate blog traffic.

And so, as promised, this is my third and final blog on lil' Adolf.

A completion of a trilogy – inspired by *The Lord of the Rings*, but without any of the substance or literary merit – whose parts basically have nothing in common with each other except my ranting about the ding-a-lings who named their son after Adolf Hitler and a reference to an esoteric beverage dispensing appliance.

I've given a lot of thought as to what I could write that I haven't already made up about a 3-year-old with seriously stupid parents. Frankly, there's not much. So I leave you with this poem:

Ode to Adolf

Dearest Adolf, oh so young
It's not your fault
That your parents
Have brains of dung

They named you poorly
After an infamous Nazi
And now New Jersey
Has you in protective custody

We hope that state
Will change your name
To something that is not
Quite so insane.

Like Jeff or Bob
Or Jack or Ted
Some name which doesn't
Brand you, a skin-head

Life is tough
And life is long.
Naming you Hitler.
Was just plain wrong.

Some day, when
You're of age
I hope your heart
Is not full of rage

Forget your namesake
Was a dictator
And have a draft
From your Kegorator

Church Foreclosures On The Rise

Originally Posted Wednesday, December 31, 2008

I was reading in the *Wall Street Journal* last week how a church building boom that began in the 1990s is resulting in some foreclosures in the current economic downturn.

This brings up an interesting question.

If you are the banker who holds the note on a church that defaults on their mortgage, and you – as said banker – chooses to foreclose on the financially delinquent church, does this get you an express ticket to Hell when you die?

I would imagine that foreclosing on a house of worship would be a rather big black mark on your soul, which no amount of goodness could overcome.

Saint Peter: (looking over your stats at the Pearly gates just after you died) *Let's see, you tithed every year from the time you were 12 until you passed. Very, very good. You donated thousands of hours to the under-priviledged during your lifetime. Excellent. Hmmm, what's this? You became a banker and foreclosed on a church? I guess on the bright side, it wasn't YOUR church. That would have been very, very bad. This is just bad. The down escalators are to the right behind that cumulonimbus cloud. Next!*

According to the WSJ article, many of the country's 335,000 churches carry little to no debt, but some churches "borrowed briskly to build or expand" in the decade from 1997 to 2007. Last year alone, construction spending on houses of worship nationwide was $6.2 billion. That's a lot of pews.

But then the economy tanked and suddenly church members were not donating as much weekly or fulfilling their commitments to building campaigns. One church in Florida that avoided foreclosure by filing for bankruptcy collected only a third of the money pledged for a $1 million building campaign.

I guess that church didn't have a Ministry of Guido.

Guido: (knocking on the door of a delinquent parishoner) *Duh boss sez youse is behind on youse pledge for the new wing of the church. He sez youse pledged a grand, but have only given two bills. I'm here to assistchu in finding those missing C-notes.*

It's not surprising that people pledged this money, but then failed to come through in the end. After all, we haven't had an economic melt-down like the one we're living through since the Great Depression.

Unfortunately, when many people have to choose between Eternal Salvation or a 57" Sony Widescreen TV with 1080i resolution, high definition will win most of the time.

Besides, it makes the most of that Blue Ray player you just got for Christmas.

A Blog Where I Don't Complain

Originally Posted Wednesday, April 21, 2010

It was recently pointed out to me that I complain "a lot" in this blog.

I was going to complain about that observation, but realized that would be completely in character, so instead I will cheerfully agree.

It's actually true. Although, if you think about it, since the name of this blog is *The Irony of It All* one could assume that a certain amount of complaining is practically a requirement. Synonyms for irony include sarcasm and satire, which can easily be construed as complaining.

In person, I rarely complain about anything. Well, OK, I do have a habit of growling at bad drivers, but that's not so much as complaining as venting. After they are no longer in my purview, the venting stops.

But in this blog, I do complain a lot.

For instance, I complained about the recent $40 million school bond issue in Cape Girardeau. Actually, I did that several times dating back to December when the first rumblings of the bond issue surfaced. Most of the entries were sarcastic satire, although I did explain my reasons for not voting for the bond issue in one of the offerings.

I also complained about the census and how wasteful it is sending out letters telling people their census form was going to show up the next week then following up the census forms with post cards.

That advertising campaign was apparently not successful. I just heard that only a third of the census forms were returned by the government deadline. Good thing the census bureau sent out all those notices or I bet nobody would have sent their forms in at all. Damn! There I go complaining again, using sarcasm. When will I learn?

I did reflect on why I complain a lot in this blog – apart from the whole "irony" issue – and came to the conclusion that a lot has to do with how I make my living.

I work with computers on a daily basis often troubleshooting problems. After doing this type of work for 20 years, I've come to realize that it is extremely rare for technology to work exactly as expected or as promised. There is always some hidden "Gotcha!"

I'm of the opinion there is a downside to practically any technology. I expect things not to work as advertised and that's what I often sniff out. I'm like a negativity truffle-hound.

And as a result of doing this daily at work, I constantly look for the "Gotcha!" in everything in life. Things are not all sunshine and lollipops and if it looks too good to be true, it probably is just that and this truffle-hound will sniff it out.

But in an effort to not be so gosh darned negative, I'm going to dedicate the rest of this blog to being *positive.* That's hard for me, considering the whole negativity truffle-hound aspect of my personality that I previously explained, but I'm going to give it the ol' college try.

For instance, I will admit that I have been critical and a wee bit sarcastic of the new Cape Girardeau trash system that the city will start using in May.

I've made fun of the name of the service (C.A.R.T.S.) calling it lame. And I wondered about what would become of the poor trash men who had always dreamed of being trash men and were now being put out of work by a robot. And I also questioned the practicality of the system operating in some of the older parts of town.

Complain, complain, complain, that's all I did.

But even though the new trashcans are very big – that's not a complaint, I'm just stating a fact – I kind of like them. Unlike any of the trashcans that I currently own, there is _not_ a single hole in the bottoms of any of the brand new trashcans.

At least, not yet...

...Oh, nuts!

When Ants Won't Eat The Cat Food

Originally Posted Monday, July 12, 2010

How bad is cat food when ants won't even eat it?

This thought crossed my mind the other morning as I was clearing the two paper plates on our front porch that I'd put out the night before with cat food on them for Smokey, our nephew's cat.

A little background is in order.

We have a cat – Patches – that we feed half a can of "wet food" every evening. While we have experimented with various kinds of wet food, she seems to like Fancy Feast the best. Now that doesn't mean she eats the entire half-can we put out for her. She essentially laps up all the gravy, nibbles on the rest and leaves most of the food on her plate for us to dispose of.

Disposing meant throwing it away, but then about 2 years ago, my wife decided that we were wasting perfectly good cat food and gave the leftovers to Smokey who tends to loiter in our front yard and for good reason. Her owner – our nephew – lives next door.

This communal cat feeding has evolved into an evening ritual where we give a quarter of a can of wet food to our own cat and the rest to Smokey on a paper plate that I pitch the next morning.

While our brand of canned cat food rarely varies – Why fix something if it is not broken? – I did recently experiment with some new offerings from Fancy Feast. They were introducing flavors just for "Gravy Lovers." That describes our cat to a T, so I picked up one of each of the available flavors to test.

Sure enough they appeared to have more gravy, but Patches hasn't been terribly excited about any of them. She eats her usual amount of gravy, and then wanders out to our sunroom to study the bird feeders from her carpeted perch.

Smokey was another matter. She has not touched any of her portion of the three "Gravy Lovers" that I have put out for her. She sniffs the contents and looks up at me as if to say "This is what I've been waiting for ALL DAY?"

So when this situation occurred last Friday, I succumbed to that woeful look and put a second plate of food out for Smokey, sitting it on the porch stairs just above the offensive entrée. Smokey had no issues with that plateful – Grilled Chicken in Gravy – and devoured all of it, leaving just a few specks of meat.

However, rather than pitch the plate of "Gravy Lovers" food, I decided to leave it out overnight in case one of the other neighborhood cats wandered by looking for a bite to eat.

That apparently didn't happen, or if they did, they were in agreement with Smokey on the quality of the food.

The next morning the "Gravy Lovers" plate was still sitting where I put it the evening before, completely undisturbed. But I couldn't help noticing a line of ants that was ferrying the crumbs from the other plate back to their nest out in a nearby flowerbed.

The line went right by the first plate, but the ants ignored it as if there was nothing there worth eating.

That observation made me wonder:

How bad is cat food when ants won't even eat it?

Dear Doofus 'Parked' In The Passing Lane

Originally Posted Tuesday, August 17, 2010

I know that you're from out of state. That is obvious.

You have Tennessee license plates and stenciled on the back of your packed white passenger van is the name of an Assembly of God church from a city in the Volunteer State that I've never heard of. Since you're from out-of-state, I should probably cut you some slack.

And I should also cut you some slack since you are – after all – a church van and that would be the Christian thing to do. Perhaps, there is a bible-verse that says something to the effect that you should let the man pass who has the large team of oxen pulling a heavy load. If there's not, there should be. That is part of my own personal philosophy.

For instance, if I'm entering a convenience store and the representative from the local Budweiser distributor is trying to deliver a loaded two-wheeler, I will not only get out of his way, I will gladly hold the door open for him.

I believe you should _always_ hold the door for the beer man. It's the right thing to do.

And I feel the same when driving on the interstate. If you had been in a hurry, and wanted to pass me, I would have moved out of the passing lane and let you by.

But you weren't in a hurry.

In fact, you were in front of me cruising along in the passing lane. Perhaps you don't have these things in your state. That's what we call the far left lane of the interstates in Missouri – the passing lane. It is the lane we use to pass other slower vehicles. The system works quite well.

The passing lane is a very simple concept.

When you are driving on the interstate – I-55 in this case – you should always use the right lane unless you are passing or being a good Samaritan and moving over to allow entering traffic to merge. When you are done passing or the right lane is open for you to move back over, you move back over.

You should not drive for mile after mile in the passing lane unless you can't move over – which was not the case in your situation. While I was behind you, there were several times you could have moved over, but chose instead to poke along in the passing lane.

Eventually, the white car ahead of me had to pass you in the right lane. You would think that may have tipped you off.

"Gee, why is someone passing me over there?" you may have thought, but apparently didn't. Maybe you were too engrossed in singing "99 Bottles of Beer on the Wall" to notice.

I finally had to do the same as the white car. I don't like having to pass another driver like that, but your inattentiveness gave me no choice. Thankfully, the driver from the other church bus in your caravan was not as clueless as you.

When I passed him a few minutes later he was in the right lane where he should be. At least, that is where he should be in Missouri. Maybe that is not the case in Tennessee.

About The Author

Brad Hollerbach lives with his wife Karie and their cat Patches in Cape Girardeau, Missouri. He is the Director of Information Technology for the *Southeast Missourian* by day and a blogger by night.

Brad has been writing a column / blog under the *The Irony Of It All* name since the late 1980s although he did take a 19-year break to pursue other interests.

www.ingramcontent.com/pod-product-compliance
Lightning Source LLC
Chambersburg PA
CBHW021145070326
40689CB00044B/1134